UTAH SPORT CLIMBING

STORIES AND REFLECTIONS ON THE BOLTING OF THE BEEHIVE STATE

DARREN M. EDWARDS

THE History PRESS

Published by The History Press
Charleston, SC
www.historypress.net

First published 2017

Manufactured in the United States

ISBN 9781467119092

Library of Congress Control Number: 2016950686

Notice: The information in this book is true and complete to the best of our knowledge. It is offered without guarantee on the part of the author or The History Press. The author and The History Press disclaim all liability in connection with the use of this book.

UTAH
SPORT CLIMBING

To Niki, for all of the reasons that you already know.

CONTENTS

PREFACE

I first thought of writing this book for my master's thesis while earning my degree in literature and writing at Utah State University. But I had successfully written about climbing before, and I really wanted to challenge myself. So I wrote a spiritual memoir instead. Had I known how much work this book would actually take, it would have given me a second reason to switch topics.

I complain about the work it took to complete this project (over two years of research, most of which came from digging up primary sources), but it really has been a project of passion. I have spent over a decade of my life sport climbing. It has enabled me to grow more as a person than almost any other single activity. During this time, I have had the chance to take over one hundred people out for their first time climbing. Even with those who never went again, I could see that the experience changed them. In the space of one climbing route, a person can go through nearly every emotion possible. They can face and overcome levels of fear they've never dealt with before. They can learn to trust their lives to others and be trusted in return.

I hold so much gratitude for the pioneers who ventured out into Utah's canyons with the vision and passion to find and develop those routes. I wanted to learn more about them, and the more I learned, the more I wanted to explore and share their stories.

That's what this book is. It's a collection of stories pulled from the earliest days of sport climbing in some of Utah's major areas. It is not, and could not be, a comprehensive history. Rather, I approached this as one of my writing mentors, Chris Cokinos, might have: as part journalist and part poet. My goal was not just to tell their stories but to reflect on them and see what they could tell us about what it means to be human.

Some of these stories, like the development of American Fork Canyon, are well known. There I have tried to provide the most accurate telling to date. If nothing else, I wanted this book to get it right. Other stories seem completely unknown. Logan and Maple Canyons are good examples of stories that may be new to even the most die-hard Utah climbers.

It is important to make it clear that this book deals exclusively with sport climbing. Trying to tackle Utah's trad climbing and mountaineering history would be its own overwhelming task. I will leave that task to someone else. I look forward to reading that work.

I had a number of audiences in mind while writing this book. First, I wanted to write it for the climbing community, to record a history that might otherwise be lost to time. Second, I wanted to write this for the non-climber so that he or she could enjoy learning from the rich history these climbers have created. Lastly, I hoped to create something of beauty for the literary community.

For the uninitiated, the language and terminology involved in rock climbing can be a bit intimidating. This presented a unique challenge for the writing of this book. How do you explain the climbing shop speak for the non-climber without boring the climber to death? So, rather than explaining what a red-point is the first time it comes up in each chapter, I've created a small glossary of climbing terminology at the back of the book. My hope is that this tool will aid the average person as he or she enjoys this fascinating piece of Utah's history.

A few notes: I've italicized the names of specific climbing routes but not the names of crags, walls or canyons. Route names are almost always followed by a parenthetical that contains the climb's difficulty rating (all ratings are given using the Yosemite decimal system) followed by a comma, the letters FA (first ascent) and the name of the climber/s who claimed the first ascent. Most routes are also accompanied by an endnote that provides readers with the guidebook the information was pulled from.

The Yosemite decimal system is used to rate the difficulty of a route. The system is divided into five types of activity, from walking and hiking to rock climbing. All sport routes would fall into category 5. The 5 is then followed with the difficulty of the climb. When I started climbing, anything below 5.10 was considered a beginner route. After 5.10, the difficulty grades further subdivide into a, b, c and d. So, a 5.10b is one grade more difficult than a 5.10a. After 5.10d, the next designation would be 5.11 and so on. The general feeling among the climbers I knew or spoke to in the 1990s was that 5.12 marked the start of expert-level routes, with 5.13 and 5.14 serving as even higher benchmarks. The end of the scale continues to change as climbers push the boundaries of the sport.

To any and all climbers who feel hurt that they weren't interviewed for this project, congratulations, you have very successfully taken yourself off the grid, and I apologize I didn't have the strength, time or energy to track each and every one of you down.

I hope you enjoy reading this history, and I look forward to seeing my recording of it torn apart on Mountain Project (which I figured would happen no matter how I did it).

ACKNOWLEDGEMENTS

I would like to thank Niki Edwards, without whose support this book (and pretty much everything I've done for the past five years) would not have been possible; Sandy Edwards, who got me through high school, a monumental task, and always supported my creative endeavors; Jerry Edwards, for teaching me the importance of doing things the right way and instilling in me a work ethic I would not otherwise have; and my siblings: Curry, for keeping me open-minded; Jenn, for midnight fry runs and always welcoming me into your home; and Special-K, for helping me survive the other two. To all of my nieces and nephews (Grahm, Aiden, Alex, Johna, Miles, Beck and Luci), thank you for keeping me young. To my son, Michael Dean Edwards, you were only weeks old as I finished up this project, so I won't hold my lack of sleep against you.

I would like to thank my editor Artie Crisp and The History Press for their understanding in granting me multiple deadline extensions as I continued to stalk climbers, trying to set up interviews.

This book would still be an idea in my head without the help of hundreds of climbers, from beginners to masters, who helped with the research that brought this project to life. Thank you to those people who helped me connect the dots and make contact with the climbers whose histories I was writing. I appreciate everyone who allowed me to barge into their afternoon of climbing and let me photograph them. I stood on the shoulders of several guidebook authors while researching this project (James Garrett, Stuart and Bret Ruckman, Tim Monsell, Todd Goss, David G. Robb, Casey Hyer, Karl

Kelley, Dave Pegg, Sibylle Hechtel and Josh Holmes). Also, a large thanks goes to Matt Driscoll for the work he did with the Outdoor Recreation History Project.

Thanks to the over sixty people I interviewed for this project. For all the work they've done in developing rock climbing in Utah and for sharing their stories with me, I owe an immeasurable thanks to climbing icons James Garrett, Bill Ohran, Boone Speed, Bill Boyle, Jeff Pedersen, Mike Anderson, Mike Pleinis, David G. Robb, Noah Bigwood, Lisa Hathaway, Todd Goss, Scott Datwyler, Matt Cupal, Jason Stevens and Vince Adams, among others. And to everyone else who allowed me to visit with them—Morris Attwell, Susan Bosse Attwell, John Ibach, Scott Bushman and others—thank you!

I owe my deepest gratitude to a long line of educators for teaching, inspiring and mentoring me: my third grade teacher, Ross Durrant, who recognized and went out of his way to encourage my desire to write, and Laurel Shelley, from American Fork High School, for teaching me more than she knows (and for not failing me when I probably deserved it). From Utah State University, I'm humbled to be able to thank Michael Sowder, Charles Waugh and Brock Deither for sharing the craft of writing with me. Chris Cokinos and Jennifer Sinor, I can never express how much your mentorship has done for me. And special thanks go to Star Coulbrooke, who taught me the meaning and importance of a creative community.

To anyone I've ever shared a writing group with—Niki, Daniel Nyikosh, Elizabeth Benson, Jacoba Poppleton, Kaci Lundstrum, Braden Lindstrum, Russ Beck, Chadd VanZanten, Adrian McBride (RIP) and Chelsi Linderman, who was insane enough to start a weekly open-mic with me—thank you.

To anyone who's ever been a part of the Storm the Mic community—everyone at Jazzy's, Ron Coulson, Kayleen Williams, Kathy Hawkes, Hanna Morgan Davenport, Adam Gigi, Ryan Ruthkowski, Savahna Jade Owen, Ashley Bushy, Devin Asher (RIP), Sky Flower Warburton, Dallen Terril, Lex Spafford, Alex Hardy, Ammiee Olsen Cox, Elaine Willson, Gabrielle Yivone, Joel Lewis, Alicia Walker Farrie, Elaine Jean Westerguard, Kim Bentley, Maria Cazares, Zack Maki, Susan Kower Beasterfield, Christina Osborn, Brit Ishiem, Roman England, my dear friend Marian Hales Harding and so many others I don't have room to name—your words and friendship have kept me going for years.

To everyone involved in the broader southern Utah creative community—Melynda and Amy Marie Thorpe; Elise West; Ryan Gruskowits; the incomparable Janice Brooks; the Heritage Writers Guild; the entire English department at DSU; Eric J. Reed, aka the Merch Monger; Virgina Griener;

Dave West; Dawn Laliberte McLain and the entire St. George Book Festival committee; the Kayenta Arts Foundation; Garry Morris and Kent Harris, two of my all-time favorite people; Megan O'Sullivan and Mathew Burnette at Main Street Books; Lisa and the late Tim Cretsinger, who started Groovefest; Josh Warburton; and so many others—thank you for inspiring me.

An extra special note of gratitude goes to my teammates on the 2014 and 2015 Southern Utah National Poetry Slam teams (Erika Larsen, Whitney Shirtleff, Janae Godfrey, Lauren Jo Sypniewski, Gina Grissom, Michael Jergensmier and Ron Coulson).

I'm sure that there are many, many more people I should be thanking; please forgive me for not having the room to mention you all.

Lastly, to all of the climbing partners I've had over the years (Seth Haddock, Judd Shelton, Jake Taylor, Chris McQuivey, Josh and Becca Ingersol, Emily Marsh, Jamie Snyder Mcfarland, Lauren Jo Sypniewski and so many others), thanks for the belay and/or spot—and not letting me die.

INTRODUCTION TO SPORT CLIMBING

What is sport climbing? This can be a simple question with an equally simple answer. Sport climbing is a form of rock climbing that utilizes fixed metal anchors (bolts) to protect a climber as opposed to free soloing (climbing with no rope at all) or traditional, "trad," climbing (placing temporary, removable protection like nuts and cams into cracks or other natural features within the rock). A sport climber, with the assistance of a belayer, follows the route created by these small metal bolts up a cliff face. Usually, the end of the route is marked with a set of chains, from which the climber may self-rappel or have his belayer lower him. As one route developer told me, sport climbing simplifies the safety aspect of climbing, freeing up the climber's mind and body, allowing them to attempt more acrobatic, athletically demanding moves. Climbing is a broad term. Climbing Mount Everest has as much in common with working on a bouldering project as Riverdance has to do with break dancing. Respectable in their own rights, they have little in common. Generally, rock climbing is broken down into four subcategories: bouldering, sport climbing, traditional (or trad) climbing and big wall.

Sport routes (climbs) are created by dedicated climbers who, in nearly every case, are paying for the materials out of pocket with no hope of compensation or income. These are esoteric, creative adventurers, and it shows in the names that they give their climbs. *License to Thrill*, *Monkey Brains*, *Teenagers in Heat*, *Vomit* and *Screaming Lobsters* can all be found in American Fork Canyon. I like to imagine the confusion any non-climbers must have when they overhear a snippet of a conversation between two climbers.

"Yeah, I took a total whipper on *Suicide Blonde*, but the day got better when I jumped on *Gorillas in the Snow*."

"That's awesome! I totally flashed *Gorillas in the Snow*. We should go try *Narcolepsy*."

Despite having its own language, sport climbing seems more accessible to the average person than the gear-intensive trad climbing or the high-risk field of free soling. Even bouldering (climbing short routes, usually on boulders, that are highly technical and require exceptional strength), can scare people off more easily than sport climbing. This is why Jeff Pedersen, a renowned Utah climber and owner of four successful indoor climbing gyms, puts the bouldering section of his gyms in the back or on the second floor. You don't want the Olympian-like gym rats scaring off the first timers who have come in for family home evening (a Utah/Mormon tradition of dedicating one night a week to a family activity), or Boy Scouts, or a first date. More and more often, these are the places and ways people are getting introduced to sport climbing. Climbing is no longer something that only the most adventurous of adults can enjoy. I was first introduced to sport climbing back in the 1990s at the first climbing gym in Provo, Utah, a little hole in the wall called the Rock Garden that sat just off Center Street in Provo. We were there for a Boy Scouts activity.

While a laughing family or a pair of hormone-crazed high schoolers wandering into a gym and giving sport climbing a try doesn't require any imagination these days, back in the 1980s, it would have been unheard of. And the '80s is when sport climbing really started to gain some solid footing in the United States.

Invented by French, German and Italian climbers, sport climbing changed the way the world looked at rock climbing. While the movement was initially met with scorn in the United States, climbers eventually began to see the effect this new form of climbing was having on the technical abilities of the French, German and Italian climbers. Slowly, the movement would find a place in the States.

With the invention of "sticky rubber" shoes, climbing company Boreal allowed climbers to attempt routes up rock faces that they never would have tried before. When people hear the term "sticky rubber," they usually picture shoes that stick to the floor. Sticky rubber isn't sticky in the way that gum or glue is sticky. It's a material that holds more friction than the conventional rubber you find on your tennis shoes.

The invention and advancement of power drills likewise played an indispensable role in making sport climbing a mainstream activity. Before the invention of the Bosch cordless power drill in 1984, anyone who thought about placing bolts into a cliff face for protection would have needed a generator and a long power cord or, much more likely, a hand drill and a lot of time. After their invention, cordless hammer drills set climbers free to drill bolts as far into the woods or desert as they'd like with much less effort. Of course, those first cordless drill batteries didn't hold much of a charge before the climber would have to return home to give the battery more juice. So, many climbers made "turbo" packs—homemade battery packs that were much heavier but lasted longer. I'm told Bill Ohran was a master at this.

In 1983, Alan Watts put up what is considered to be the first sport-climbing route in America, *Watts Tots* (5.12b, FA Alan Watts) at Smith Rock in Oregon, though, it's worth noting that people like Hank Armantrout and Drew Bedford had established a handful of sport routes up places like Ferguson Canyon in Salt Lake City during 1983.

As sport climbing gained more followers, it also met more resistance. Trad climbers holding to the old-school climbing ethic felt that there was no place for bolts or, at the very least, no place for bolts that had been put in on rappel (rap bolting). If you were going to put a bolt in a route, you'd better climb to that bolt's spot from the ground up using traditional protection. No dangling from a top rope looking for the best bolt placement. No rehearsing the climb or figuring out its moves before trying to claim the first ascent.

When sport climbers refused to adhere to these standards, things could reach a boiling point—like when things nearly came to blows between climbing icons Ron Kauk and John Bachar at the camp four parking lot in Yosemite. Longtime friends and former climbing partners, Kauk and Bachar had both become outspoken about their conflicting thoughts on climbing ethics—Bachar anti–rap bolting and Kauk pro.[1]

Things rarely went as far as they did at camp four. What was far more prevalent was the practice of chopping bolts. After someone had established a sport route that someone else thought crossed their ethical line, it wasn't unusual at all for the offended party to grab a hammer and crowbar, head up to the cliff and either pop the bolts off or just smash the bolts' hoods flat. These kinds of conflicts are generally referred to as the Bolt Wars. While most areas have evolved beyond this type of behavior, there are still a few spots where it's said to happen.

To outsiders, this conflict may seem petty or trite, but climbing has never been a small thing to those who do it. For many people, climbing is a lifestyle. It's what they breathe. They work whatever jobs give them enough to survive and allow them the free time to climb as much as possible. And it's not just a young person's life. In fact, most of the hardcore lifers that I know are older climbers. These are people who have found ways to stay active in a dangerous and physically taxing activity well into retirement age, often at an incredibly high level. For them, climbing is life, and the ethical issues surrounding it, from bolting ethics to environmental impact, are no small matter. For some of them, sport climbing ripped the soul from traditional climbing. It was an abomination. Where was the adventure? Where was the sense of discovery and losing oneself in the wild? To the sport climber, the answer was in the athletic and challenging technical nature sport climbing provided.

Like most simple things, the answer to this question (What is sport climbing?) can become remarkably complex when looked at from the right angle. In part, that is what this book does. It takes the simple details of a history and explores them, tilts them this way and that in hopes of finding what is beneath the surface. This is one of the reasons that I've picked such a narrow focus for this work. A comprehensive history of sport climbing in Utah would fill volumes and lead to dozens of arguments over accuracy, regardless of how it was written (the world of rock climbing has no shortage of controversy, disagreement and conflicting stories; indeed, I've found that we can't even reach consensus on how we feel about the existence of such disagreements). A comprehensive history of rock climbing in Utah as a whole would challenge the set of encyclopedias that sat on my childhood bookshelf. But by focusing on a handful of stories from the earliest days of sport climbing in nine of its most popular regions in Utah, I was left with enough space to lay these stories out on the dissection table, peel back their layers and examine some of the themes that sit at the heart of not just sport climbing but the adventure of being human.

1
IBEX

The places we wish to remain protected and wild cannot become so unless [they are] visited and appreciated
—*Richard Bangs*

James Garrett, author of *Utah's West Desert*, told me the story of his first trip to Utah's West Desert over lunch at a chain restaurant several hours south of Notch Peak, near my home in Washington, Utah. Our hostess, a young woman I imagine must be a student at the local university, Dixie State, was kind enough to move us to a back corner table in a closed section of the restaurant. Garrett was just passing through town between climbing trips and charity work. I imagine this is what most of his life is like at this point.

With the clatter of utensils clanking against plates playing softly in the distance, Garrett explained, "I had seen a picture of the north face of Notch Peak in Michael Kelsey's hiking guidebook to Utah." For someone who seems to thrive off adventure and even more so on discovery, the picture was all it took to lure Garrett down from the Salt Lake area out to the West Desert, at that time an area known for only sheepherders and its connection to the Pony Express.

Garrett has existed in the outdoors for most of his adult life. After graduating with a degree in liberal arts (political science), he opted not to go to law school. Instead, he became a member of the first Big Sky ski patrol in Big Sky Montana. He was one of nine men who covered an area now patrolled by nearly two hundred individuals. "It was our mountain. Every

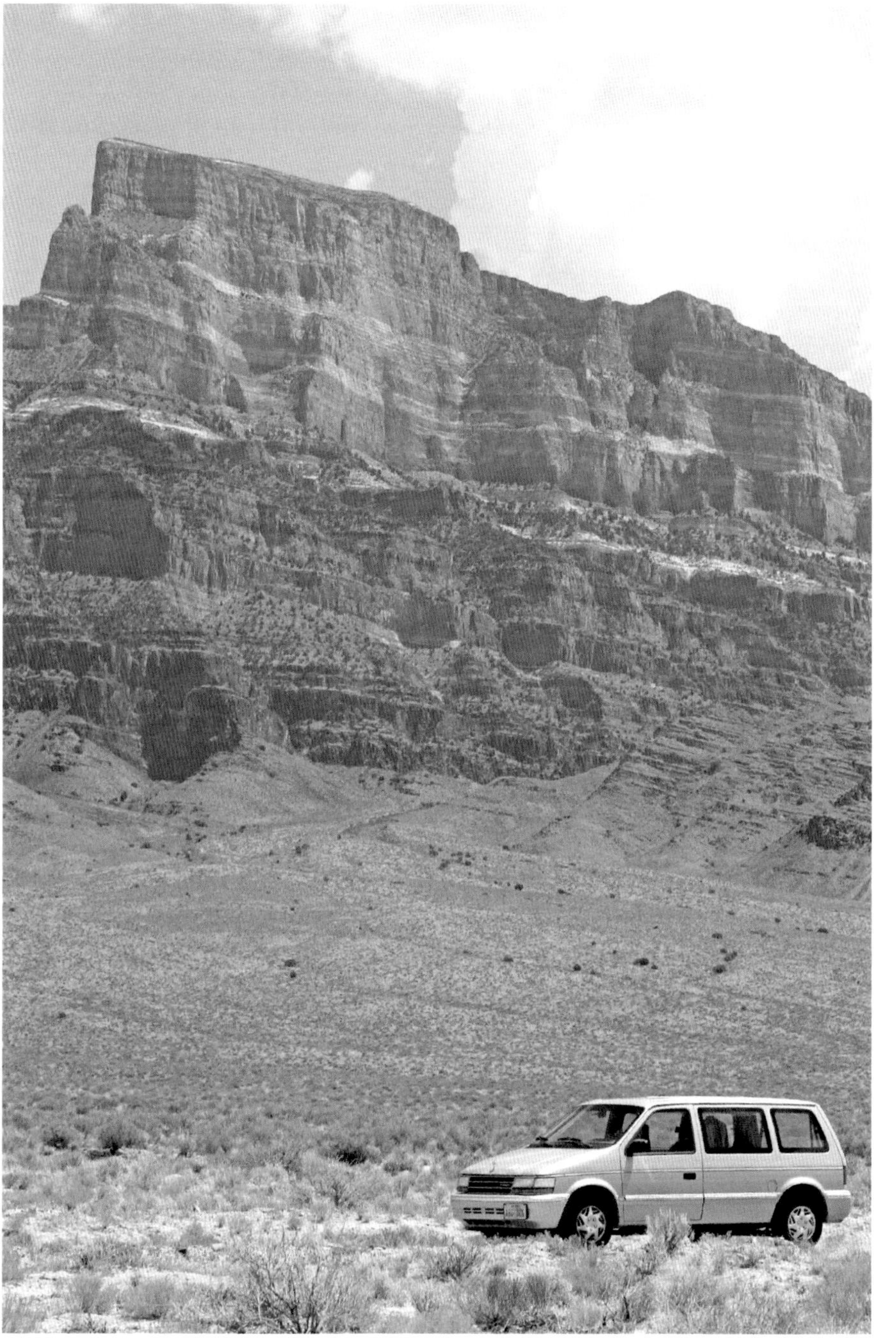

We approach Notch Peak in my wife's old van. *Author photo.*

run that we skied was a first ascent. We were naming them. It was a beautiful time," Garrett recalled with a smile.

While his fellow guides were already rock climbers, Garrett didn't really dig into climbing until he moved to Switzerland for a five-year stint between his first and second years working at Big Sky. There, surrounded by the dramatic peaks of the Swiss Alps, he experienced his first real taste of rock climbing. "I ended up meeting Dougal Haston, one of the most famous Scottish climbers. He did the first ascent of the west face of Everest with Bonington," Garrett noted. Haston, a climbing legend with cavernous eyes and wild hair, showed Garrett where the local quarry was. Before long, Garrett was setting up top ropes in that quarry. It was also during his time in Switzerland that Garrett met Jürg von Känel, the first Swiss climber to tackle a 5.13. Through his example, von Känel would teach Garrett a lesson that would influence his climbing style forever.

Once von Känel broke into that 5.13 range, a difficulty level I can only dream of, he decided he'd gone far enough. Rather than push his own level further, von Känel began hunting down and developing more accessible climbs that emphasized enjoyment over difficulty. As Garrett put it, "His whole focus turned to putting up what he decidedly called *plaisir* ["pleasure" routes]. He basically decided, 'I'm going to put up long, moderately rated, well protected bolted climbs.' And he started, almost, a revolution." In other words, plaisir routes are climbs established for the pleasure of climbing as opposed to their difficulty.

This notion of plaisir climbs comes through in the routes Garrett himself has developed. While he has put up some astoundingly difficult climbs, such as the five-pitch *Shadow of the Jihad* (5.13a, FA James Garrett and Tim Toula), he has also developed some of the easier, most-loved routes in the state, like the single-pitch *Sheep in a Wolf's Clothing* (5.8, FA James and Franziska Garrett).[2] And these routes make the truly unmatched experience of venturing up into the vertical world available to a broader portion of the public, a notion not everyone agrees with.

Some argue that the type of experiences you can find letting your soul hang out on the rock should be available only to those who earn them. As much as I might like to, I cannot say that this idea is invalid. But does a fleet of soccer moms top-roping a bolted route diminish the experience of the person who free solos it? I can't say. Still, I struggle to picture the advanced climber thinking about anything other than the moment they're living in when they're on the rock. See, that's one of the reasons I love climbing. As humans, our brains run like twenty-four-hour mini marts. It seems we are always in our own heads. We are self-aware to a fault. Our subconscious is self-conscious to the point that even when the mini mart is empty at 2:00 a.m., the lights are still on, and the teenager with bad teeth and a neck tattoo is still standing behind the counter flipping through his selfies. With climbing, though, the lights go out, and we lock the doors. These are pure moments, the rare moments we long for where we don't feel the weight of our past or the pull of the future. We are, in these moments, wrapped entirely in sense. We don't analyze the moment. We live in it, really live in it. Annie Dillard, who I can't seem to help but quote, calls these moments "gaps." They are the gaps in our self-consciousness, moments of pure unselfcontiousness. I think that is why I hold so much admiration for the developers of sport climbs. Without necessarily intending to, these developers have made it possible for people who might not otherwise experience the gaps, the unselfconscious moments climbing provides, to grow from the self-discovery that can be found in them.

There is something about the places where we find our gaps that becomes almost sacred, and the more people who find their gaps out in nature, in our public lands, the better shot we have of protecting those lands from dangers like development and mining.

I imagine Garrett found his way into some of these gaps during his time in Switzerland. His experiences in that quarry sparked something inside him that has never quit burning. Sitting in that corner booth, working our way through lunch, Garrett noted, "Very quickly, I started ice climbing, mountaineering…but being a real rock climber, that didn't happen until I came back from Switzerland, and I settled in Utah."

The move to Utah in 1981 came with some pleasant surprises for Garrett and his wife, Franziska, whom he'd met while in Switzerland (and whom he describes as the best climbing partner he's ever had). They'd come for Franziska's medical residency at the University of Utah (U of U). The quality of the mountains and the climbing were a benefit they'd not necessarily expected.

The Salt Lake climbing scene was still small, but locals had already established a plethora of classic traditional routes in Big and Little Cottonwood Canyons, and as early as 1983, people like Drew Bedford, Hank Armantrout, Bill Cramer and Dave Casey were bolting sport routes.[3] Careful to respect the work that had already been done, Garrett tackled as many of these classics as he could before he started putting up his own routes. He said, "I think that when you climb in an area, especially in the United States, where there's a lot more climbers, I think that when you go to a place you need to get a feel for the place, and by getting a feel for the place I mean do some of the existing routes…I think there is something inherently wrong with going to a place and not doing any climbing whatsoever [then putting up new routes]."

During this period of "becoming local," Garrett enrolled in classes at the U of U, where he eventually obtained a nursing license. This enabled him to explore the world in exciting new ways. Pausing between bites of his burger, he explained, "With a nursing license I worked in Papua New Guinea for Chevron. They flew me back and forth, business class, every five weeks." While most people might be in a rush to get back to the States, Garrett turned layovers into an art form. "I could climb anywhere…and I was paid for it…I'd go climbing in Thailand. I did a new route in Malaysia, [the] Kinabalu area, with my wife. I went climbing everywhere basically. Everywhere in Asia. I went climbing in Africa. I'd work out round-the-world flights so that I'd leave work and maybe go to Kenya via India. I did some climbing in India and Nepal. So, that was a great climbing job."

The average American might struggle to identify most of these places on a map. Hell, I had to look up where Kinabalu is. But here is a man who has not only been to them and climbed in them but also put up first ascents in most of them. He developed a climbing wall right outside Kathmandu,

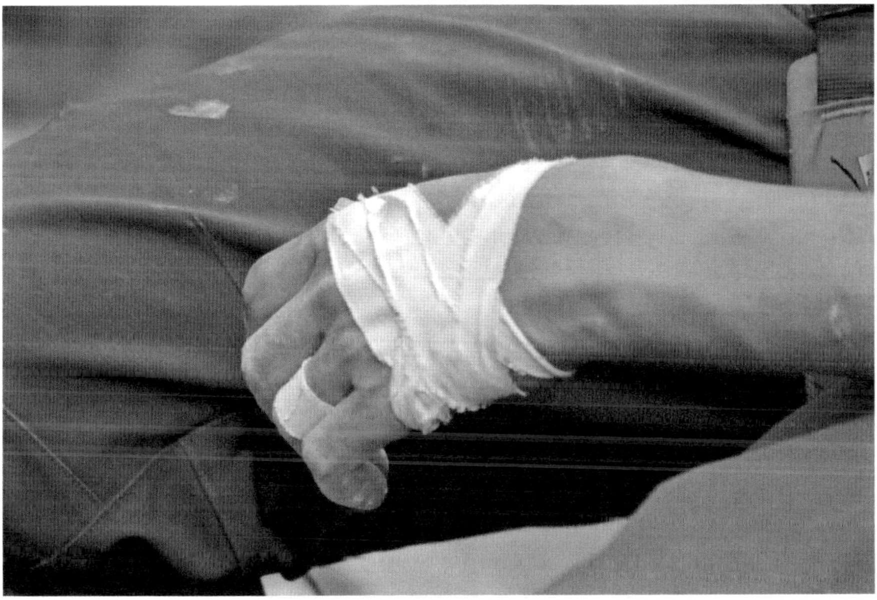

A climber rests his hands wrapped in athletic tape. *Author photo.*

where he also helped set up a new intensive care unit (ICU). He worked in Haiti after the earthquake. Some of his nursing efforts were done simply as volunteer work. He worked with Doctors Without Borders. This man has lived anything but a normal life. He has lived the kind of life I've listened to at least one hundred students sit across from me and describe as their dream. Yet when I asked him if there was something special about him, something different from the average couch potato, nine-to-five weekend warrior or soccer mom, his sincere and humble reply was "I don't feel myself as special. I've had a great life. I don't have any regrets." Then after a moment of thought, he conceded, "I guess that's pretty special, not to have any regrets. A lot of people live with regrets." The accomplishment then was not the amount of climbing done, not the skiing and not the first ascents but chasing after the things that you want with an enthusiastic determination. As Annie Dillard put it, we should be chasing these things down "with a fierce and pointed will."

It was this enthusiasm for discovery and new experiences that, years ago, put Garrett in the seat of an old Toyota Corolla en route to Utah's West Desert and the then unclimbed Notch Peak and Ibex area. Notch Peak, an impressive wall of stone that stretches up to the sky reminiscent of a medieval fortress whose walls were designed not only to protect their inhabitants but also to intimidate anyone who might think of approaching them, sits a fifty-minute drive out from the small town of Delta, Utah. Already having cut his teeth as a local by this time, Garrett had now started establishing his own routes, including several multi-pitch classics in the Salt Lake area. The trip went smoothly, but by the time he and Tom McMillen—a man who, Garrett notes, "had done hard routes on El Cap at seventeen"—had driven down from Salt Lake City, they knew there wasn't enough daylight left to make it to the base, so they parked where the trail became too rugged for anything running without four-wheel drive (a statement I decided to test one afternoon in my wife's twenty-five-year-old Chrysler van—Garrett hadn't exaggerated!) and started looking for a place to camp for the night. "There was an old mining cabin right at the entrance of West Saw Tooth Canyon" Garrett recalled as our server brought him a cup of coffee. "It was open.... We didn't have to break it open or anything." They planned to rise early and test out the peak the next day. While the cabin might have offered some protection from the elements, it came at a cost. The cabin's previous tenants, a nest of mice, kept the two climbers up most of the night by crawling around and over them. "In retrospect, we should have just set up a tent," Garrett said before taking a sip.

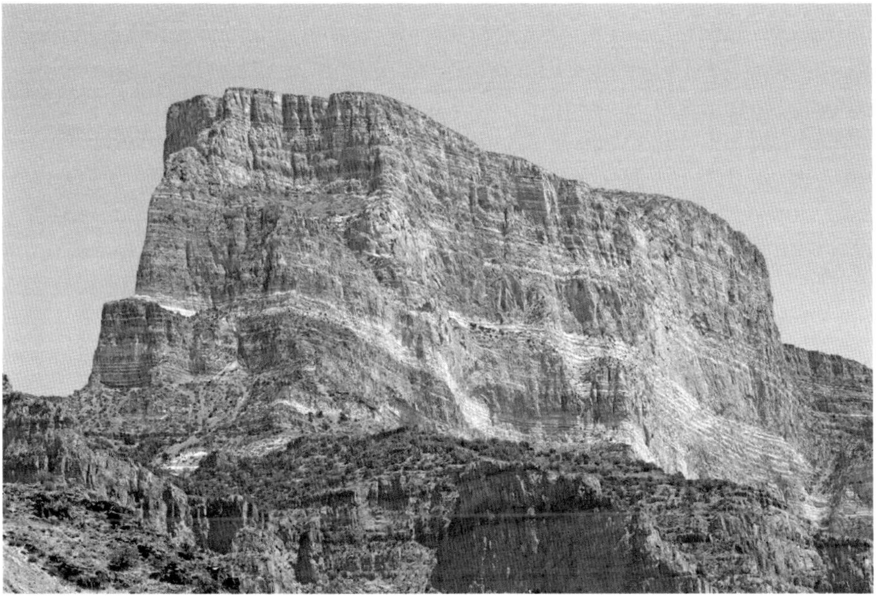

Notch Peak looms over the desert, West Desert, Utah. *Author photo.*

When the sun rose, it took them three hours of hiking to reach the base of Notch Peak. That left them only enough time to do a couple of pitches before the day was mostly gone. As they lowered back down, the vantage point showed Garrett a sea of granite. He would return later and not only claim the first ascent of Notch Peak but also establish many other projects in that granite sea.

Garrett made trip after trip to develop climbs in West Saw Tooth Canyon. The battery life of those older drills wasn't what it is today, and a day of bolting a route ended when the drill's battery life did. The jaunt back to Salt Lake to recharge was not a short one. Every trip to and from West Saw Tooth would have taken Garrett past Ibex. The highway cuts right between the two sections of desert, Saw Tooth to the right, Ibex to the left. Still, the thought of exploring Ibex (the area, perhaps, he is best known for) never occurred to Garrett. In fact, every time he looked to the left on his drives, he thought, "This looks like total choss. Who would bother with that?" Fortunately, Garrett's good friend Patrique Maloney pressed matters one trip, assuring him that it looked like the kind of place he knew Garrett would love to explore. So, abandoning their plans in the shadow of Notch Peak for a day, Maloney and Garrett turned right toward Ibex. Even at thirty feet away, after crossing the Tule Hardpan, a stretch of hardened ancient seabed, he was still convinced that Ibex was bad rock. He figured he'd touch it and say, "It's choss. Let's turn around and go to West Saw Tooth." But when they reached out to feel the face of those Eureka and Watson Ranch Quartzite cliffs, they knew instantly that it was some of the best rock they'd ever touched. So they didn't turn back to West Saw Tooth that trip. Instead, they started putting up, on lead, the route that would become *Severity Disparity*, a bolted two-pitch climb that jumps from a 5.10a on the first pitch to a 5.11a on the second pitch, the first route ever bolted in what is now the West Desert's most popular climbing destination. Garrett did only the first pitch on lead that day with Maloney. He would have to come back the next weekend and rap-bolt the upper pitch.

This new section of the West Desert kept calling Garrett back. I imagine this had to be an unusual experience for someone so drawn to discovering new places. Talking about a friend of his who frequented one area of Greece almost exclusively, James said, "I would never go anywhere nine times, with the exception of Ibex, where everything was unclimbed. Every time I went out there, I'd put up a new route." Still, despite the tremendous amount of work Garrett and his various climbing partners have done, and despite all the route development they've inspired other climbers to do (enough to fill several hundred pages of guidebook), there is still lifetimes' worth of climbable rock to be explored in Utah's West Desert. As Garrett says in *Utah's West Desert*, "Whole areas wait idly to be discovered by the adventure climber." And perhaps thanks to one particular afternoon of developing plaisir routes out at Ibex, the land will still be accessible for those future climbers.

Garrett and a climbing partner were just lowering from a climb when they saw a group of large earth-moving machines headed toward them. The mining group had easily acquired a permit from the state to take as much of the quartzite as it wanted.

By the time the two climbers had reached the bottom of the cliff, the miners had already moved their machinery into place. "When we got down there, we just tried to have an upbeat attitude and tell them, 'Hey, we cherish this area,'" Garrett recalled. He handed out some of the old guidebooks he'd made for the area and told them, "This is our playground. We love this place."

The climbers continued to stand around and talk to the miners for some time before the man in charge of the miners said, "Yeah, I think that's pretty cool. We've got other places to go. We can go someplace else."

While I'm sure they didn't feel it at the time, and may not feel it even looking back on the experience, the image of two climbers standing in front of a full crew of miners, big machinery in tow, trying to convince them to

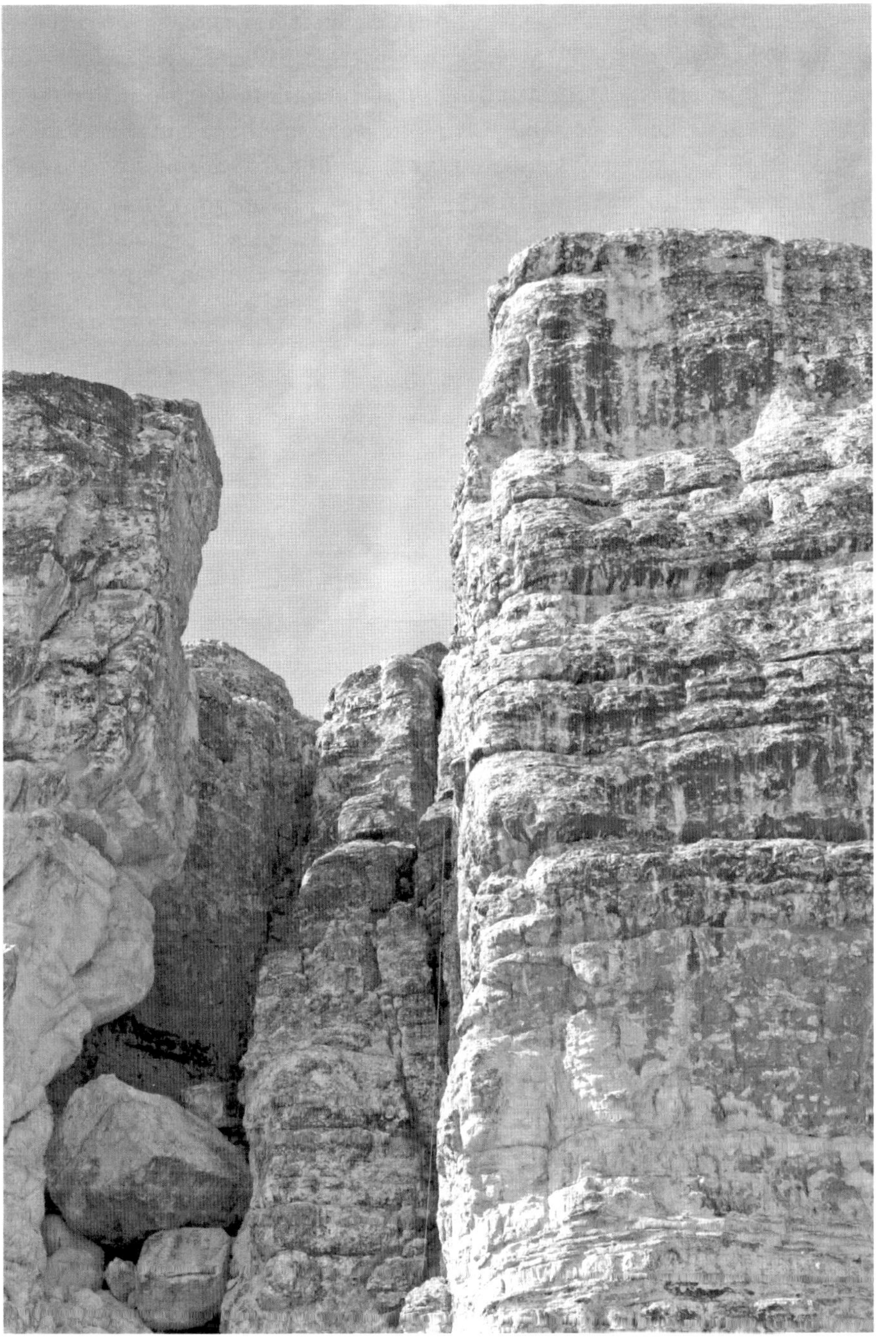

An unknown climber works his way halfway up a route at Ibex. *Author photo.*

leave a cliff face intact is one of the gutsiest things I can picture. It's also an image that seems to lie at the heart of the way Garrett climbs and approaches guidebook writing. As Garrett said to me during our lunch, "If we keep these places secret, we have to ask ourselves who we're keeping them secret from. It's certainly not from the mining companies and the developers."

It's by loving the land and the ways in which we can respectfully use it—and being willing to share that love with others—that we can build what *Outside Magazine* founder Tim Cahill calls "a conspiracy of caring."[4]

2
SNOW CANYON

I have lived in southern Utah for six years now, and it can be difficult to see this landscape as anything other than what it currently is, a thriving community of around 150,000 people that has been carved from a red rock desert. But if I try, I can think back to the early '90s, vacationing in a small town that was just starting to develop. The first time we made the four-hour trip south from our American Fork home to see the St. George timeshare my dad had bought into, we laughed at the directions we were given.

"You'll wrap around the bluff until you hit the big dirt hill that has a kid playing on top of it. That's when you turn left."

That's how I remember the directions being given the morning we started the trip. My parents must have assumed that they'd know where to turn because of the dirt hill, the kid playing being a bit of a flourish on the part of our guide. But that evening, to our surprise, there he was, nearly five hours after the directions had been given, playing on top of a mound of dirt.

My friend Janeene, who has lived here much longer than I have, remembers driving down St. George Boulevard (the main drag) and getting stuck behind people who had decided to park in the middle of the road, get out of their cars and have a conversation. People drove tractors and cattle anywhere and everywhere in town. During the early '90s, something changed. The secret got out, and the area started to develop at an accelerated rate. As John Ibach, former Snow Canyon State Park manager, noted, "It was the fastest-growing city its size in the nation for many, many years." Now, the St. George area is a sprawling series of cities and towns, and St. George Boulevard can be bumper to bumper regardless of the time of day.

While most people would argue that this transition has been a positive one, it hasn't always been a smooth one. St. George and southern Utah went through (and in many ways are still going through) their share of growing pains. Some of those pains were felt in Snow Canyon State Park. When Ibach took over as the park manager for Snow Canyon in 1993, the area was just starting to experience this commercial and residential boom. As the city grew, its foothold in the tourism industry grew to match. Ibach was in charge of managing the land in a state park that was under increasing demand. Horseback riders, ATV users, hikers, wedding planners, film companies and little families wanting to have a Saturday afternoon picnic all felt entitled to use the canyon. Everyone, it seemed, had a use for the glorious red and tan striped bluffs. Perhaps my favorite example is the Segway company that wanted to open up business in the canyon—because, you know, hiking is easier when you don't have to move your feet.

One group of users had managed to go unnoticed (whether a blind eye was willfully turned or not is up for debate) by Snow Canyon's previous managers. Climbers had been in the area for around a decade. Sandwiched between Zion National Park in Springdale and Red Rocks in Vegas, the area, which holds hundreds upon hundreds of hidden climbing spots itself, was ideal for big wall climbers, but it wasn't until the early '90s, several years after the rest of the state, that climbers started bolting sport routes.

While the northern portion of the state remained remarkably free of the type of ethical conflicts that the practice of bolting presented to climbing communities across the country, Snow Canyon was rife with them. From climbers removing (chopping) bolts to deface another climber's route to chipping off or gluing back on handholds, everyone had their own way of seeing things, and their way, it would seem, was the only way. As Ibach noted, "There was never anybody that could settle on a common ethic or a common theme or a common safety feature. It was always a contention. Every climber, especially the ones that do the bolting, had an idea of what that route should be, and that route is sacred. You can't alter it. You can't touch it. You can't climb it in a different way."

Ibach recalled a few instances where a route developer stood at the base of a climb yelling at a group of climbers, demanding that they come off the wall because they weren't doing it correctly. While these conflicts never turned violent, the possibility was always there. Sitting across from me in his office, while my recorder ran, Ibach said, "I mean, there were climbers in there with guns that the other climbers were afraid of. All because they were crazy. Tape it: they were unstable characters." It's hard to picture a group of climbers walking up to a route, gear in tow, excited about the possibilities the afternoon could hold, stopped short by some self-deputized climbing enforcer with a gun. A little bit of the old West had sauntered into Snow Canyon.

Exploring the mindset of such climbers, Ibach explained, "The climbing community is a really funny community. It's something that I wasn't familiar with because I came from a boating background. I'd never dealt with climbers. I just kind of figured they were people that you could talk to." He paused to laugh then added, "And you know, in some respects they are, but in some respects they're not....For them, it's like the last great American freedom, and they're not going to be messed with. That's their freedom, and they don't want to come to the table."

Todd Goss, author of *Rock Climbs of Southwest Utah & the Arizona Strip*, recalled things a little differently. Goss found his way to St. George by sheer chance, literally a split second of it. He'd been climbing at Red Rocks in Las Vegas and was headed north on I-15. While he was passing St. George at sixty miles per hour, something caught his attention. "I look over and I see this sign that says 'Climbing Equipment' on the side of a building that's facing the interstate," Goss recalled. "To this day, I don't know how I made the turn. Somehow, I managed to turn off into the outdoor outlet." What Goss would find was a more welcoming community of climbers than he'd ever encountered. That same day, he left the outdoor outlet with a handful of papers that were the closest thing to a guidebook the area had and another piece of paper with five names and numbers of locals he could call to go climbing. "Anyplace else I'd ever been the locals were sort of territorial and not really very welcoming....That was unique." Goss used a pay phone to call one of the names on the list, Bo Beck, and the next morning, they were climbing in Snow Canyon.

The area grabbed Goss. His plan had been to leave Red Rocks and spend the winter in Tucson, but the landscape and climbing possibilities kept him in the St. George area. Seriously, he just didn't leave. He lived on public land by Gunlock Reservoir, a patch of blue surrounded by red rock and contrasting green trees, for the first few weeks until he met another climber, John Sisil, living in the back of his car at the Green Valley Gravel Pit. John's boss at the construction company where he worked had given him permission to sleep in his car at the gravel pit to keep vandals away. By vandals, I mean a certain climber no one would give me the name of who, in a bit of radical environmentalism, had decided to set a tanker truck of diesel fuel on fire.

In a scene straight out of *Myth Busters*, the tanker exploded, causing over $1 million in damage.

Teaming up with Sisil, Goss brought his trailer to the gravel pit, and he and Sisil lived there for around a year as the gravel pit's "custodians." Goss got a job as a server at a local restaurant and spent his free time exploring the area.

At the time that Goss started climbing in Snow Canyon, he recalled, only around ten real climbers were doing anything in the area, and there were maybe seventy climbs in the canyon, all trad or bolted on lead. The existing developers—Ron Olevsky, John Tainio, Matt Kindred and Mike Anderson among them—were still in the older-ethic mindset that all bolting needed to be done on lead. As Goss pointed out, "Snow Canyon's not a very cracked place. It's mostly varnished-face climbing. They started to do, even by today's standards, really bold bolting on lead, runout, slab, friction stuff."

I recall the first time I climbed in Snow Canyon. My friends and I were used to climbing the steep overhangs of American Fork Canyon, so when we first looked at the climbs in Snow Canyon, we mistakenly thought they'd be easier. We'd never climbed anything where every move was based in friction and every bolt was runout. In American Fork Canyon, if you fall, you drop through the air for a bit as the slack between you and your belay partner whips out. In Snow Canyon, if you fall, you're looking at scrapping, slamming and banging your way down as the slack whips out. And these climbs came with a lot of slack. Goss hit it on the head when he said, in reference to those original Snow Canyon climbers, "These guys must have carried their balls around in a wheel barrow."

Here is an interesting contradiction. According to Ibach, these climbers didn't feel the need to acknowledge the authority of park management—didn't want a new, more hands-on manager telling them what to do—but at the same time, it was their desire to bring Ibach into the middle of their conflicts that brought the climbing community to his attention in the first place. While many aspects of the southern Utah climbing community were peaceful and welcoming, it wasn't at all uncommon, according to Ibach, for him to find one climber or another standing in the parks office complaining that someone had messed with their route or stolen a rope they'd left at the top of a climb.

Ibach noted, dryly, that he had "climbers coming to [him] and saying, 'I left some rope over there and it got stolen. What are you going to do about it?'" And, he'd point out the obvious, "Don't leave it there. That's your property; don't leave it." For Ibach, who admits it took him years to even get familiar with the terminology in climbing, there was little incentive to jump into the middle of these disagreements. Still, they were taking place in a state park under his stewardship. As Ibach put it, "They probably felt like they were in my sights right away, but they brought that attention upon themselves. If it hadn't been for the infighting amongst themselves, who knows, they might have gone unnoticed for five years, but it was pretty hard to ignore them." This is not to say that all of the climbers developing routes in Snow Canyon during the early '90s were equally responsible for the problem. Though their relationship may have gotten off on a rocky note, climbers like Goss, Dean Wood and others eventually became a valuable resource for Ibach.

Goss conceded the point that Ibach must have seen climbers as a thorn in his side during those first few years of his tenure at the park—especially, he noted, with the conflicts that would arise between Ron Olevsky and John Tainio.

Speaking of Ibach, Goss said, "John's amazing! He made a statement at a meeting we were at one time. He said, 'Bolts are not impact. People are impact.' From a land manager at the time, in the '90s, that was just…you could have knocked me over with a feather kind of thing. That was really enlightened I think."

While Ibach chose not to call the climber out by name, he did feel that a certain individual could receive most of the blame for the conflicts between climbers. "There was one individual particularly who was just a bad character…and he was the primary bolter, the primary route developer for quite a few years down here.…It was beyond difficult. I mean, he was a scary individual because you never knew which way he was going to jump," Ibach said, adding that he was glad to let this individual know he was the root of the problem. "For a couple of years, he was the primary reason that things happened the way they did…you know, the moratorium on the bolting. Whenever I saw him, I gave him credit for everything that was going on and made sure he knew that it was him." This climber, according to several sources who wished not to be named, was Olevsky, one of the pioneers of climbing in Zion Canyon.

Because I was unable to make contact with Olevsky, I considered not mentioning him in this chapter. It didn't feel right putting him in the crosshairs without giving him a chance to defend himself. But you can't really tell the story of sport climbing in Snow Canyon without mentioning him. According to the climbers I spoke with, Olevsky was a bit hardheaded and confrontational. The main conflict arose between him and the other original Snow Canyon climbers like Tainio over Olevsky's practice of making what

Goss called "creative enhancements" to the routes he developed. This could be anything from knocking a piece of rock off to drilling a finger pocket in a flat, varnished face to make a climb a bit easier.

After hearing and reading so much about Olevsky, it occurred to me that he did make an easy target. He was seen as gruff and idealistic. He climbed with a 9mm handgun strapped under his shoulder. The front image of an interview with Olevsky in the April 2004 issue of *Rock and Ice* featured Olevsky pointing his 9mm directly at the reader. In a time of shifting climbing ethics, Olevsky's ethics were his and his alone. Still, Goss felt that time might vindicate Olevsky. "If you look at a route like *Black Massacre*, it's three pitches of beautiful hard, varnish-face climbing. It's beautiful. In its natural state it's probably 12b or 12c. If no one ever touched it with a drill, it's probably 12b or 12c. Ron couldn't climb 12b/12c so he brought it down to about 11b with the instillation of finger pockets through, really, three or four blank sections. We're really talking about seven or eight enhancements to get us through three pitches of climbing that wouldn't have been done for a very long time." No one needs to guess as to Olevsky's motives for making his modifications. He defends them himself in that April issue of *Rock and Ice*:

> *When the* North American Wall *was first climbed it was the high-water mark of aid climbing, but I've heard that recently the pin scars are so huge people are now hammering softballs wrapped with webbing into the craters. Do we have to sacrifice our classic routes to enjoy them and see where the pioneers first went? I think we should be willing to make some compromises. Sometimes a few fixed anchors or a little bit of subtle rock modification can serve to preserve a valuable experience for coming generations. On the softer rock of the desert, such results become apparent that much faster. I don't advocate scarring, but recognize that it exists when pitons are hammered into cracks. That being the case, I feel that if pitons are used then it must be with a vision of producing a hammerless route. To say that it is the next party's problem is myopic and irresponsible, the very embodiment of poor environmental policy using performance and adventure as a smoke screen for the selfishness that produces the negatively erosional process. If you use conventional nailing with no concept or intent of creating a route that will last indefinitely, and are just concerned with your own experience, then you are part of the problem, not the solution.*[5]

Of course this is Olevsky speaking years later about aid climbing. How the same mindset can be applied to drilling finger pockets in a sport climb is unclear. Even as Olevsky's ethic applies to aid climbing, the climbing community has a hard time with it. As big wall climber Mark Synnott points out in the same article, "Ron is trying to create clean climbs so that route won't get beaten into oblivion…however…chipping, carving or sculpting rock is wrong any way you slice it."[6]

These are complex ethical and environmental issues. It's difficult to say with a firm hand who is right and who is wrong. It took years for the broader climbing community to agree that bolting a sport route on belay instead of from the ground up was acceptable, and there are still climbers clinging to the old ground-up philosophy or the even older philosophy that sport climbing is neither sport nor climbing.

Fed up with the infighting among climbers, Ibach placed a moratorium on bolting new routes in Snow Canyon toward the end of his first year as park manager. It was a strong move, a slap in the face, meant to wake up the climbing community to the reality of their situation. Ibach put a notice announcing the moratorium in the *Spectrum*, the local newspaper, and word quickly spread.

Surprisingly, reaction to the moratorium was "tepid," according to Ibach. No one lost their mind. In fact, after seeing Ibach drop the hammer, as it were, Olevsky and a few others seemed to remove themselves from the situation. Still, there were those who chose to band together and fight for the sport. Climbers like Goss and Wood sent the parks office a letter detailing the compromises they were willing to make in order to continue route development in the canyon, a move Ibach found bold if a little comical.

The timing of the moratorium wasn't random. Ibach was putting together the park's first land management plan and wanted to try to get the climbing community to a point of productive communication before the plan was finished and climbers were permanently blocked from the park.

The move worked. As Ibach noted, "The outcome was beneficial because it brought more people to the table when we did our resource management plan [for them] to say, 'How are we going to continue here? Because right now we can't do anything. Let's try and figure out a way we can do something.'" Speaking of the moratorium, Ibach added, "If nothing had been done, there would have been no need for them to come to the table." Once they were at the table, climbers had a chance to really plan for the future of their community and sport climbing in the area. Speaking about Goss, Ibach said, "I've come to respect Todd because he's been here a long time, and he saw, ultimately, the value of the resource and that the long-term viability of their sport depended on their willingness to pay attention to the environmental part of what they were doing, so it wasn't just do whatever. It was do it the right way. He really tried to build a future here for the climbing sport."

And indeed, more people did come to the table. Tim Duck, who was a Bureau of Land Management ranger; Bo Beck; Wayne Harding; and Goss approached Ibach with the mindset that they weren't with the Olevsky camp or the Tainio camp; they were a third group that wanted to ensure climbing could continue in Snow Canyon. Many of these individuals, along with botanists, search-and-rescue workers and land managers, would later form Snow Canyon's first Climbing Advisory Team.

Goss recalls sitting at his kitchen table with an old topographical map of Snow Canyon and a set of colored markers and zoning the canyon from memory according to which areas had a high density of climbs, a medium density of climbs and a low density of climbs. Goss couldn't have known at the time that his colored topographical map would become almost institutionalized as a cornerstone of climbing management in Snow Canyon.

Later, Goss and others formed the Southern Utah Climbers Coalition (SUCC) to better enable them to fight for access to climbing areas. Their efforts have gone well beyond Snow Canyon. SUCC developed and still maintains Crawdad Canyon, one of the only privately owned climbing canyons in the nation, in partnership with Susan Bosse Attwell, the canyon's owner. They successfully stopped one of the area's most popular bouldering destinations, Moe's Valley, from being turned into another in a series of ever-increasing subdivisions.

The boom in sport climbing put a momentary strain on the young southern Utah climbing community. These climbers had to work through their own growing pains, but they came out on the other side better and stronger for it. Climbing ethics will most likely continue to evolve over time, but if we can learn from past examples, look to these early sport climbers for guidance, perhaps the next progression can go a bit smoother.

3
CRAWDAD CANYON

The first time I climbed in Crawdad Canyon was over ten years and forty pounds ago. I was just pushing my way into the mid-5.11s with hopes of soon trying some 5.12s (at the time, I found the general feeling among the climbers I knew was that 5.12 marked the start of "expert" climbing, and I wanted to consider myself expert really damn bad). The trip was part of a rock climbing vacation I took with a handful of good friends, a trip that ended with me nearly getting decapitated by a roof at the Green Valley Gap, a deep V carved into flat land on the west edge of St. George, Utah. Unlike Green Valley Gap, Crawdad Canyon is a wooded wonderland—a wash of greens, dark browns and blues hidden within an expanse of orange and red—dropped like some magical oasis in the middle of the southern Utah desert.

After parking in the paved lot that sits above both the canyon and Veyo Pool, climbers take a short walk down a steep road that drops them into this oasis. Shade from cottonwood trees covers everything. A creek babbles through the middle of the canyon. The air practically vibrates with bird song, and if a talking deer and bunny were to greet me with enthusiastic jazz hands—well, OK, that might actually catch me off guard. As Susan Bosse Attwell, the canyon's current owner, noted, "It's nice. It's usually at least 10 degrees cooler down here than up on top." In an area where ten degrees can make the difference between double and triple digits, that drop is welcomed.

Before entering the actual canyon, there is an entrance to Veyo Pool on the left where all climbers must check in, pay the nine-dollar entrance fee

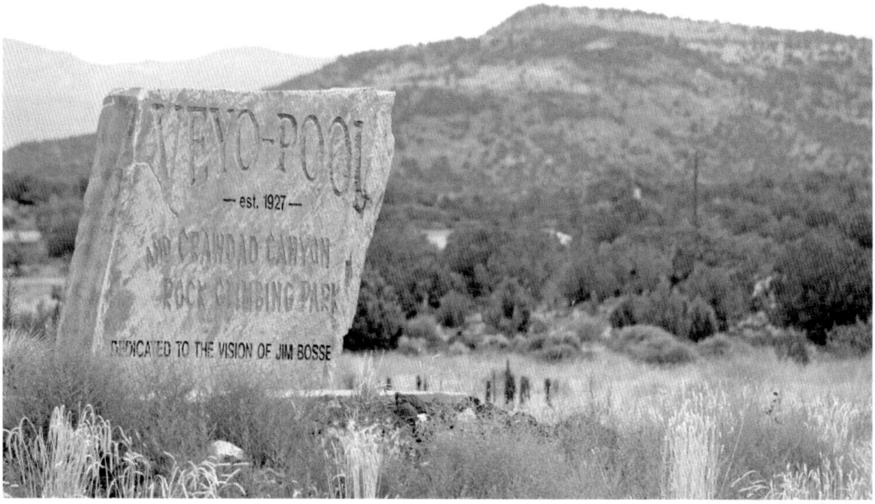

The entrance sign to Veyo Pool and Crawdad Canyon Climbing Park welcomes visitors, Veyo Utah. *Author photo.*

and sign a waiver. This is the same place climbers and sunbathers can pay for chicken strips or corn pone should the mood strike them. The canyon itself boasts over 180 bolted climbs ranging from 5.6 (beginner) to 5.13 (I can only dream about). These routes are found on dark basalt walls that can reach up to eighty feet. For the Red Rocks and Zion group, eighty feet probably sounds like standing on top of an anthill, but for a lot of us ants, that number feels just right. We—and by that, I mean me and nearly every one I've ever sport-climbed with (or bouldered with for that matter)—don't find our high from the adventure of placing gear on the eighth pitch of a seven-hundred-foot peak (though, I'd imagine that situation would also provide a very real high). We find it in inches. We find it in the challenges the stone can give us in the reach for each hold, high step, gaston and crimp, regardless of our distance from the ground.

Crawdad Canyon is one of the only places, if not the only place, you'll find route identification plaques at the base of each climb that provide the route name, difficulty rating and the name of the climber who claimed the first assent. Climbers will also find belay benches at the base of some climbs.

Veyo Pool and Crawdad Canyon are favorite destinations for locals (mostly non-climbers) and have been for around eighty years. In the summers, Bosse

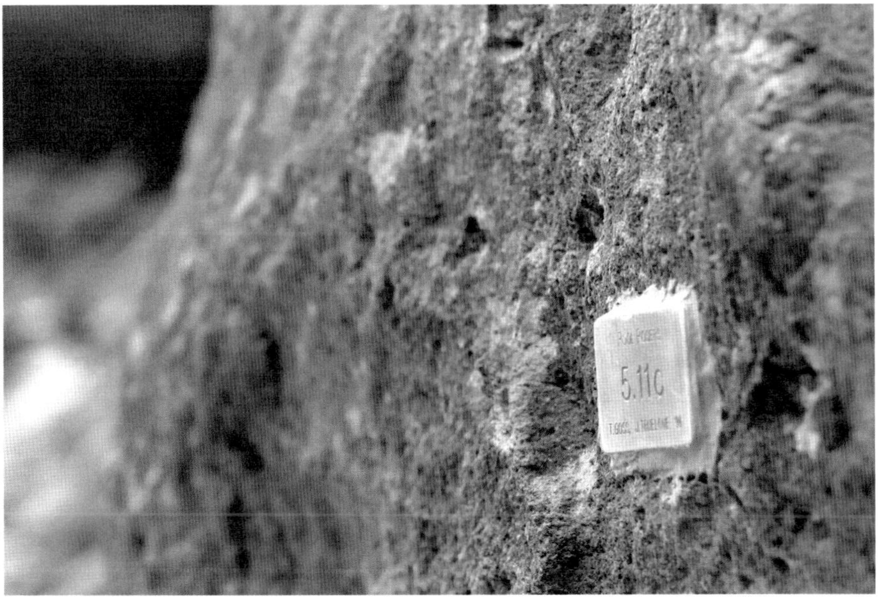

A route identification plaque provides climbers with route information, Crawdad Canyon. *Author photo.*

Attwell likes to stay at the canyon, where she can walk around, usually unrecognized, and overhear the comments campers make. She notices the children crouched along the bank of the creek trying to catch the crawdads the canyon is named for. "It's a simple thing," she noted. "There are thousands of them in there. But that's a simple pleasure at a magical age. Those things that happen at that age [kids are] going to remember forever." Time has proven her statement true. Among the things she often hears are comments made by those who are returning to Veyo Pool and Crawdad Canyon decades after their first visits, often with grandchildren in tow. She points out that all of these comments are made with a specific enthusiasm. I'd imagine it's the kind that comes from handing a piece of your past to a future generation.

The pool itself has an interesting history. Originally built by James and Caroline Cottam, its first iteration was finished in 1927. The message board outside Veyo Pool that tells its history notes that James had to do the work himself since no engineers would go near the project. Within a year of the unusual pool's completion, word spread to the point that the Cottams decided to change to pool from private to public. Over time, the Cottams added dressing rooms, an office building, a picket fence and even an orchestra pit.

"It was the happening place," said Morris, Susan Bosse Attwell's husband, a man who, for some reason, reminds me of the old Pennsylvania Dutch farmers I know.

In an area composed entirely of small towns, the Cottams' pool did, in fact, quickly turn into the social hub as barbecues and dances drew in locals. In 1953, James's son Melbourne bought him out. With the help of his brother, Evan, Melbourne expanded the dance floor, built a new, red wood orchestra pit and added a snack shop. Many young romances are said to have started at those Veyo Pool open-air dances, though, eventually, according to Bosse Attwell, the Cottams shut the social events down out of frustration at not being able to stop people from bringing in alcohol. From 1975 to '78, ownership of the pool bounced from the Cottams to Stan Meaker. Then, after Melbourne repossessed the pool, it transferred to the hands of Melbourne's daughter, Joann Balen. The pool stayed in her ownership until 1995, when she sold it to Jim and Susan Bosse.

Despite all that the Cottam family had done with the land, the canyon that surrounded the pool had gone relatively unused, with the exception of placing bits of hotdogs on sticks to catch crawdads in the creak that runs through its center. At the time, the canyon Jim bought was full of bushes and garbage tossed by some careless locals. The pool was the only attraction, but Jim

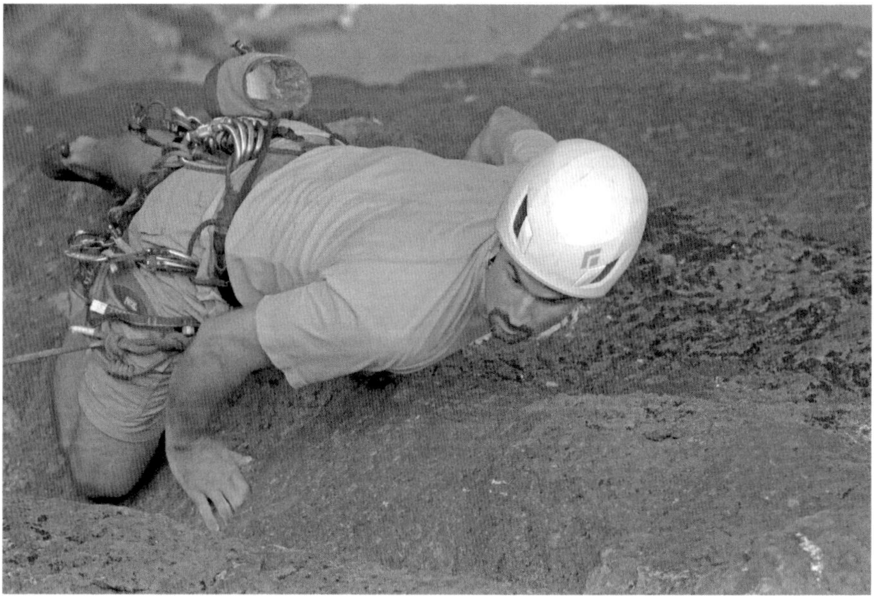

A local climber leads a route in Crawdad Canyon. *Author photo.*

saw things in a way few people can. We use the word visionary with a bit of recklessness these days (I've heard the term applied to both Kim Kardashian and Nobel Prize–winning chemist Roald Hoffman in the same hour), but Jim Bosse really fit the definition. He never saw things only as they were but, rather, as what his hands could make of them, and he would turn Crawdad Canyon into something that existed nowhere else in the country.

Usually, when a crag is discovered on private land, climbers have to hold their breath that the owners—often out of fear of liability—don't close it to climbing. See, usually, it's the climbers who have the vision, seeing a slab of rock as a doorway to a rare and challenging form of self-exploration, of interacting with nature, and it's the landowners who can have a difficult time grasping it. Their minds, understandably, fill with thoughts of lawsuits should some crazy climber dude fall on his ass. But Jim didn't just see the opportunities that fell in front of him, a task challenging enough for most of us. He hunted after new ideas the way Utah climbing legends James Garrett and Bill Boyle hunt after new terrain.

Driving around the St. George area, Jim kept seeing climbers out in the desert, clinging to steep sandstone walls. It didn't take long for him to put two and two together. He owned a canyon that wasn't being used. Climbers were always looking for new crags to develop, and the Snow Canyon bolting moratorium served as an example of the challenges climbers faced.

One day while driving past Black Rocks, small basalt cliffs sitting at the top of a shallow ravine that can be seen from Highway 18, Jim pulled over and invited a group of climbers to come check out his own little basalt canyon. Among those climbers was Todd Goss, arguably the most prolific route developer in the area at the time (today author of several southern Utah rock climbing guidebooks and owner of Paragon Adventure), and together they turned Jim's overgrown, trash-filled canyon into the first private outdoor climbing park in the nation.

There were months of digging up weeds and clearing out brush. They had to haul an old car sans engine out from the middle of the canyon, though, Bosse Attwell points out, they were careful not to change the land more than necessary. "We try to preserve everything in here that we can. We don't go cutting down trees just because they're in our way." Much as James Cottam had done with the pool's construction, Jim took on the manual labor required to clean the canyon himself. The Bosses would travel from California, where the couple lived, around Thanksgiving and Christmas to continue the work. "We would come here several weeks during the winter…in our camper, and every day we'd go out and trim and burn." The route development Jim left to Goss and the rest of the southern Utah climbing community. Speaking of the work Goss did bolting routes, Bosse Attwell said, "He has been, really, the reason why it is what it is today," though Goss is quick to direct the praise back onto Jim.

The teamwork between the Bosses and the climbing community helped Crawdad Canyon begin to rise from its own debris. Sadly, in the fall of 1998, Jim Bosse passed away. He had started something beautiful and unique. In an age when people too often can't leave well enough alone, building something mediocre on the foundation of something great, suckling off its genius to elevate their half-assed attempt to create something new—usually burying the original creation in the process—Jim took something spectacular, an oasis in the desert, a social center steeped in local history, and managed to make it even better.

Maybe that's why the bond between the climbing community and Crawdad Canyon is so strong. It's a place climbers were not only warmly welcomed to but also enthusiastically invited to help transform, to be partners in Jim's powerful vision. So when business concerns started to pose a problem, the recently formed Southern Utah Climbers Coalition (SUCC) stepped up as a nonprofit to handle the canyon's liability insurance, freeing the Bosses from the burden of that responsibility. SUCC leases the canyon walls from Susan Bosse Attwell and Morris Attwell.

This unique and, really, elegant solution to what is most private landowners' biggest fear showed the way for other outdoor climbing areas. Bosse Attwell noted that they have received many calls from both private landowners and municipalities asking how they pulled off what they have with Crawdad Canyon.

Crawdad Canyon isn't special only for the way in which it was created. The rock itself and the routes that have been developed on it are considered world class. As Morris said, "We get a lot of people from around the world coming in. We had some people from Chile…they raved about the basalt rock." Bosse Attwell recalled numerous occasions where foreigners had made the trip to southern Utah to visit Zion National Park but made sure that if they could hit only one other location on the trip, it would be Crawdad Canyon.

Many climbers from other states return year after year. That seems to be Crawdad's secret: it keeps pulling people back. Bosse Attwell told me about a neighbor who has been swimming in Veyo Pool for fifty years. Two of the Cottams' granddaughters are currently working in the snack shop, carrying on their family connection to the canyon and its pool.

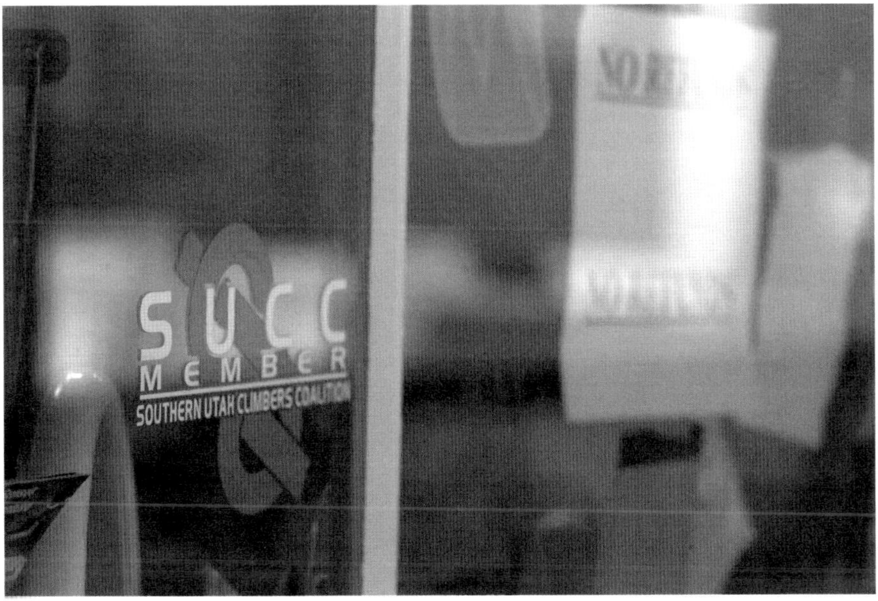

A Southern Utah Climbers Coalition sticker sits on a window, Veyo Pool. *Author photo.*

This hidden oasis in the southern Utah desert is a legacy all its own, a legacy that would have ended well before its time were it not for the vision of Jim Bosse, a vision that's helped to start changing the way private landowners across the country are looking at the relationship between their land and the climbing community.

I asked Susan Bosse Attwell how she thought Jim would feel about what Crawdad Canyon had become since his passing. "Jim," she said, "I think he'd be thrilled. I think there would have been even more directions he would have taken things." To which Morris cut in with a laugh, "Yeah, when I see 'im in the afterlife, I'm gonna whack him for not leaving some notes."

And that is, perhaps, Jim Bosse's legacy: that there is always something more that can be done—that as good as things are, if you have the vision, love and commitment to do it right, things can always be made better.

4
AMERICAN FORK CANYON

In 1850, breaking for the night, a group of Mormon settlers on their way to Fort Provo set up camp along a creek that led into Utah Lake. According to historian George F. Shelley, it was fourteen-year-old William Henry Chipman, taken aback by the beauty of the area and the stilling sense of the creek, who looked at his father, Stephen, and said, "I think I would like to live here."[7] In honesty, I can't be sure it was the creek's quiet words and the cool scent of cottonwoods and sagebrush that filled William Henry with a desire to live alongside the canyon stream; however, I have found something almost beyond calming about the way the sunlight picks its path between the leaves of a Rocky Mountain maple while a light breeze picks up the cool scent of what is now called the American Fork River.

I grew up in this canyon, fished in its river, hiked its winding trails, camped in both official and—until a park ranger's flashlight woke us up—unofficial campsites. I can't count the number of weekends I spent playing games at the Mutual Dell lodge or exploring Timpanogos Cave. The first time I ever did a misty flip was off a little snowboard jump we'd built by Tibble Fork Reservoir. From the first time I nervously led *Rockapella* (5.7, FA Brian and Vickie Smoot) at the hard rock to the time I tore muscles in my back around the corner on *Suicide Blonde* (5.11b, FA Drew Bedford), American Fork Canyon has been my favorite place to climb.[8] This canyon requires a level of strength and dynamic movement few other places outside an indoor climbing gym are able to ask.

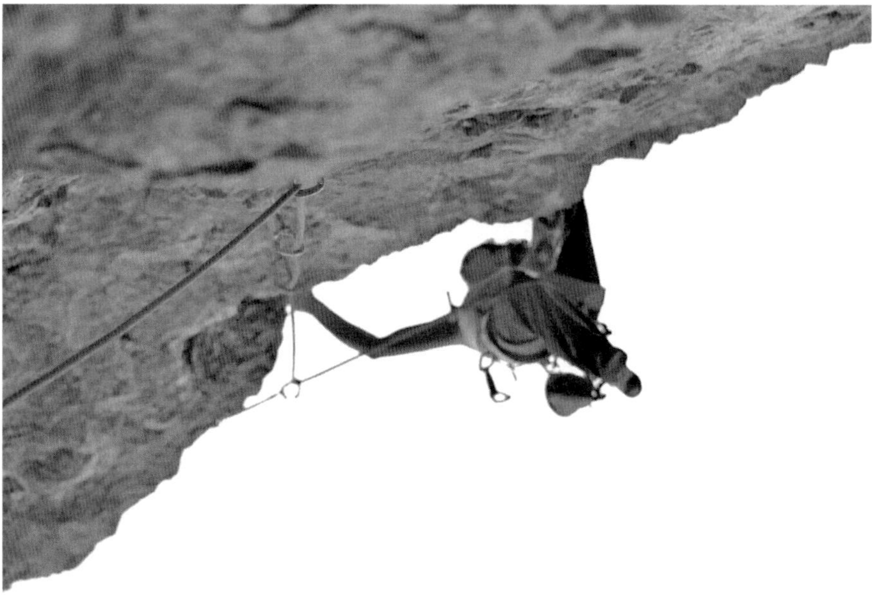

Saloni Shah finishing *License to Thrill* at the Membrane wall, American Fork Canyon. *Author photo.*

Of all the spots in American Fork Canyon that speak to me, none do so more passionately than the Membrane wall and not just because it hosts my favorite climb in the canyon, *License to Thrill* (5.11c, FA Vince Adams).[9] The main portion of the Membrane wraps you in a pocket where steep limestone reaches over you as the American Fork River rushes by your back. About a decade ago, red-pointing *License to Thrill* was at the top of my tick list. I felt that once I had conquered it, I would really be a climber. Back then, I still clung to the notion that a climb is something you can conquer, but I've since come to realize that you can't conquer a route any more than you can life. *License to Thrill* was there: powerfully, though passively, waiting for my visit, waiting to let me experience it. And it was an experience that changed me; the climb enabled me to discover something in myself and showed me that more than I thought lay within my reach.

Many people have had similar interactions with *License to Thrill.* Vince Adams, who developed the route, mentioned how he has often served as a "walking travelogue" for people and their experiences on the climb. He told me that he enjoys hearing stories of people using his route to set and accomplish personal goals. Hearing from people and seeing the excitement his route has given them helped Adams with a personal dilemma. He told me

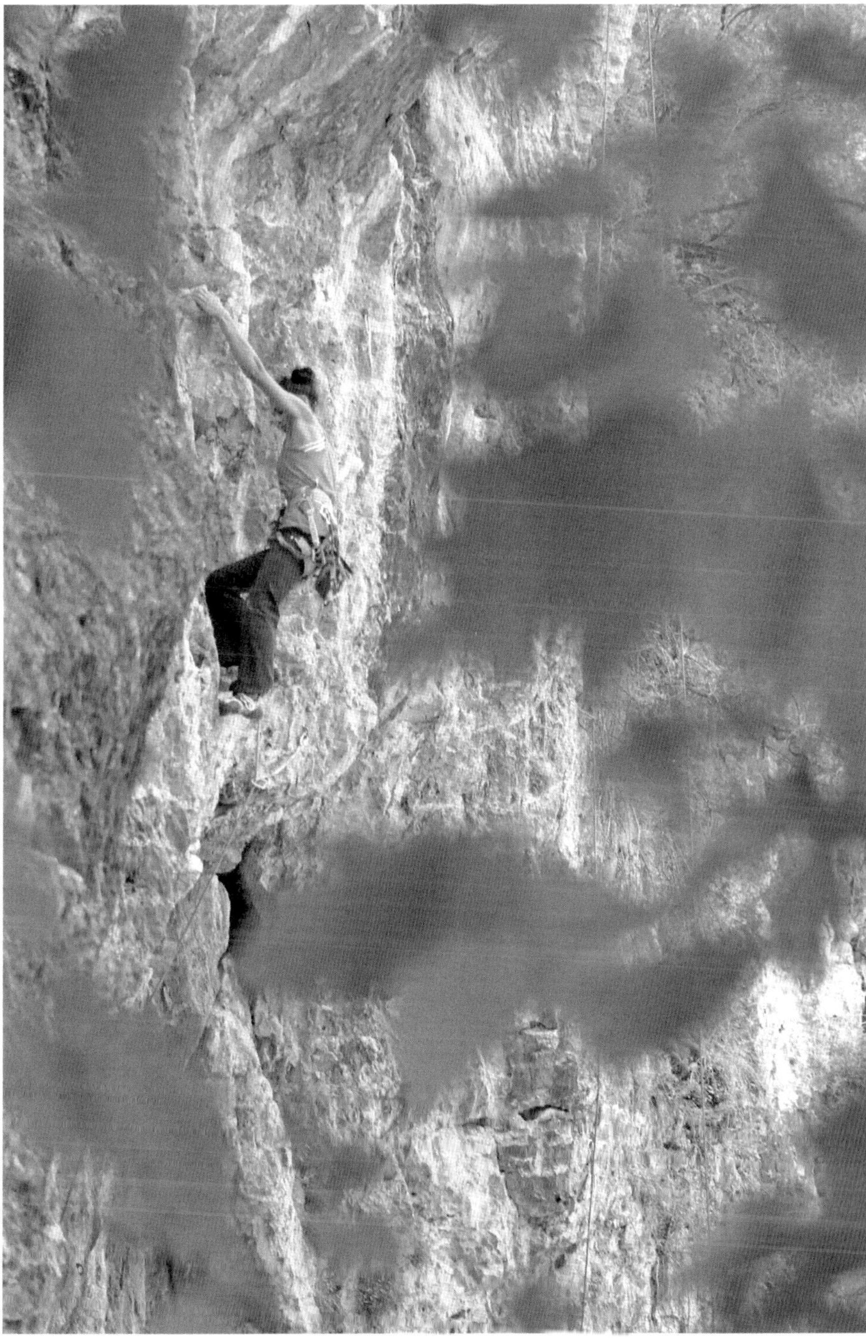

Saloni Shah halfway up *License to Thrill* at the Membrane wall, American Fork Canyon. *Author photo.*

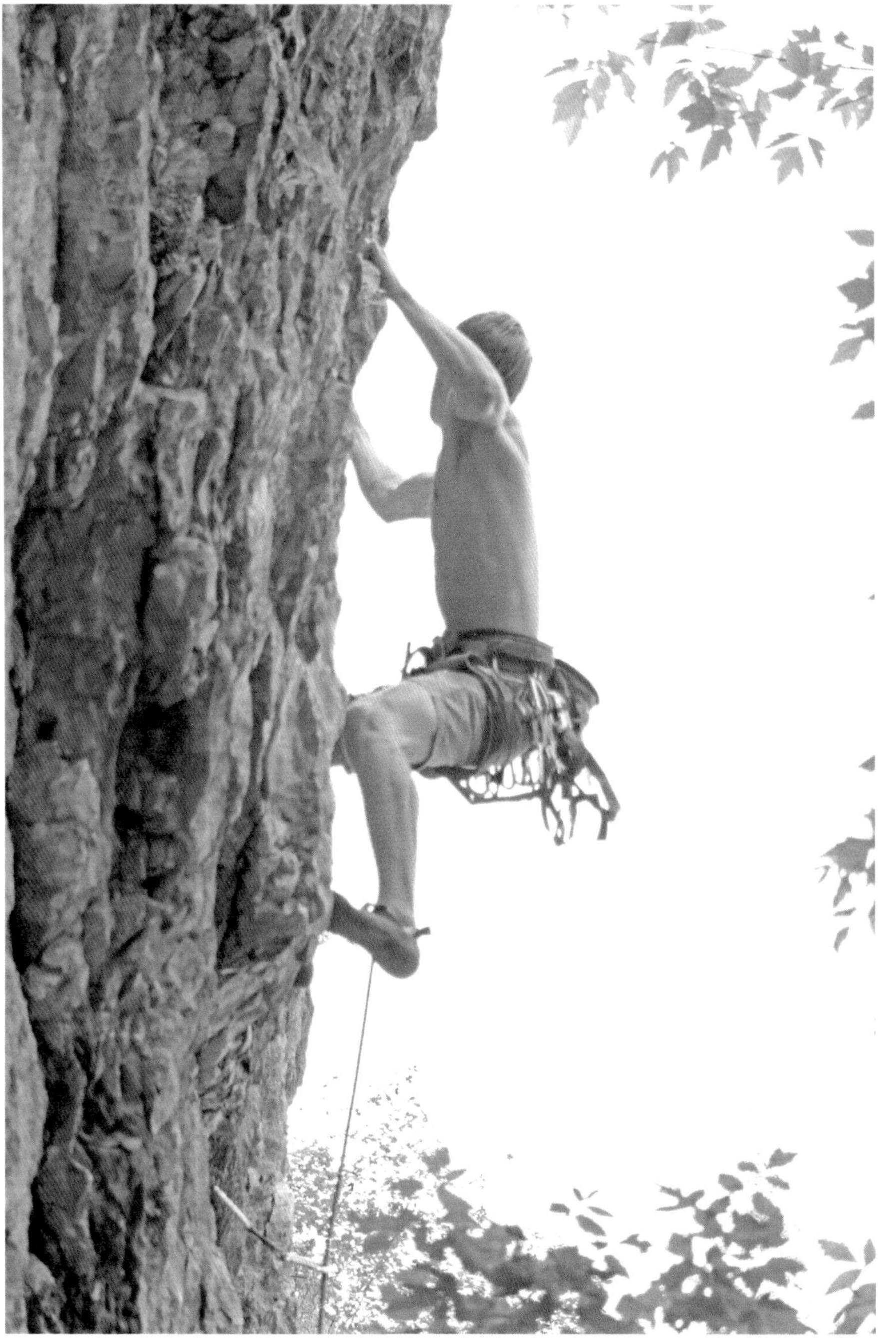

Kyle Park climbs *Rip Tide* at the Membrane wall, American Fork Canyon. *Author photo.*

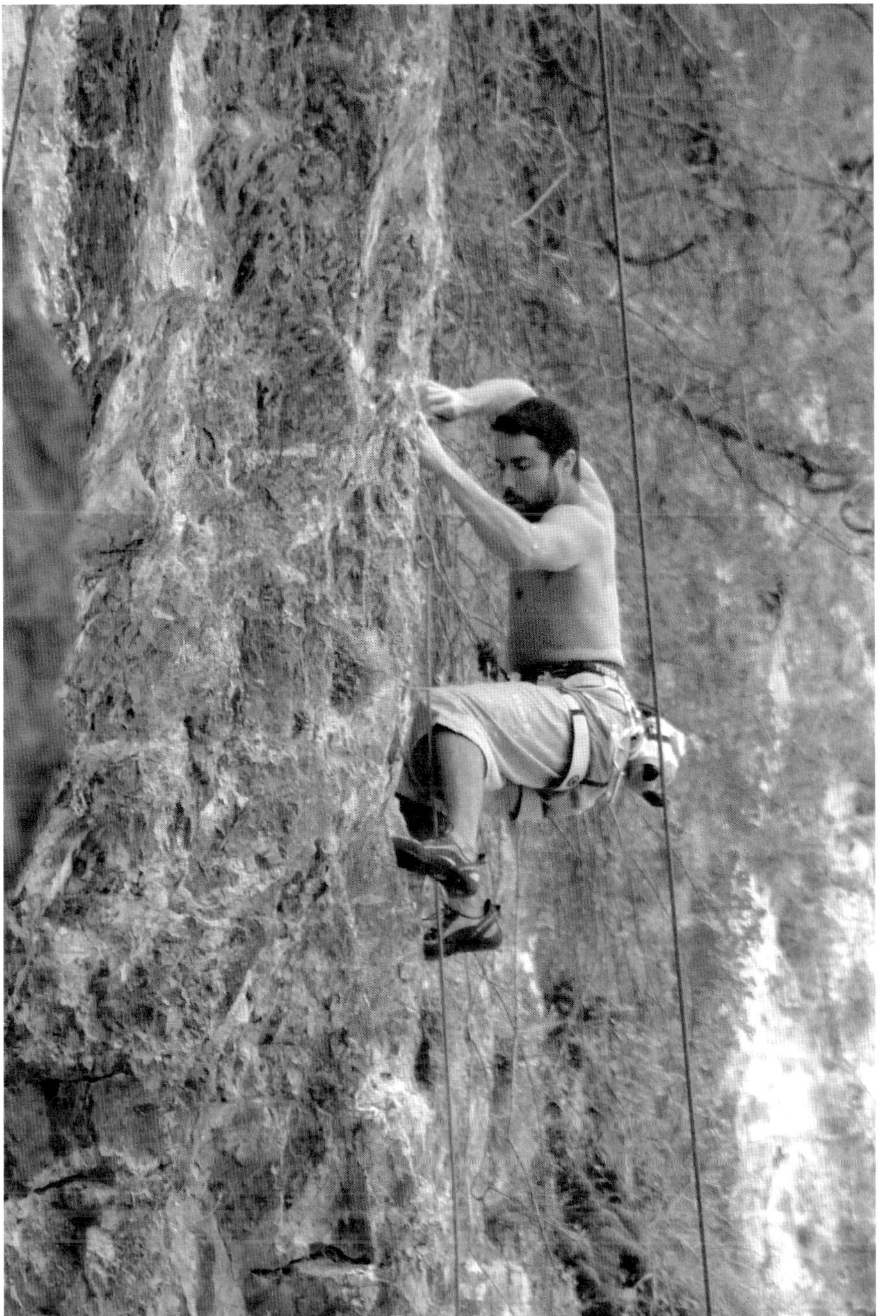

Richard Ham uses a side pull at the Membrane wall, American Fork Canyon. *Author photo.*

his struggle with climbing was that it can feel like a "pretty selfish pursuit." "I've struggled with trying to justify the amount of time that I've spent away from my family and ignoring other aspects of my life," Adams said. But he found a way to circumvent those feelings in the appreciative smiles of other climbers. "To be able to put so much time and energy and effort into something that you know somebody else is going to be able to enjoy…it's a better aspect than just going up and climbing"—not that everyone should go out and buy a bolt gun. As Adams put it, he's had "great examples of masters at bolting in Bill Boyle and Jeff [Pedersen] and the other people of that time." That time, in the early '90s, was the golden age of climbing in American Fork Canyon—a time sanctioned by visits from some of the world's top climbers (notably the Frenchmen Didier Raboutou and Jibe Tribout), who, as Pedersen said, "left their blessing on the canyon."

Boyle, Pedersen and Boone Speed are responsible not only for the development of American Fork Canyon but also for changing the way most of the world looked at bolting sport routes. These visits helped cause an American migration to American Fork Canyon.

The day I went to American Fork to get pictures for this book, I wasn't there to climb—as much as I would have liked to. I was there to get photos of others climbing. As with nearly all of my photoshoots for this book, I intentionally didn't plan anything. I just tried to catch whoever might be on the rock that day. I met two wonderful pairs of climbers, Saloni and Shaneen and Kyle and Richard. They each expressed their excitement for the routes on the Membrane wall. Looking up at the beautifully formed limestone wall, it's clear why. The whole wall is impressive; it makes me feel like a kid at the circus. Each route is as interesting and entertaining to look at now as lions, elephants and cars full of clowns were to me then. It's *License to Thrill* that gets me, though. It's the lion center stage with the tamer's head in its mouth—an interesting metaphor since I was once told that local climber Mark Davis used to stick his head in a hole near the roof of the climb for a no-arms rest. *License to Thrill* has two roofs actually, and if they don't get your attention, the first twenty feet of steep pockets will. The pockets look so deliberately placed you might think the hands of time and erosion carefully wore at each one to create the climb centuries before it would be bolted, the mountain letting it grow and develop along its surface the same way the river feeds and watches over the birch, alpine fir and Rocky Mountain maple that grow along its banks.

In reality, the hands of time had hidden the route and nearly all routes in American Fork Canyon. It wasn't until Pedersen, Boyle, Speed and others

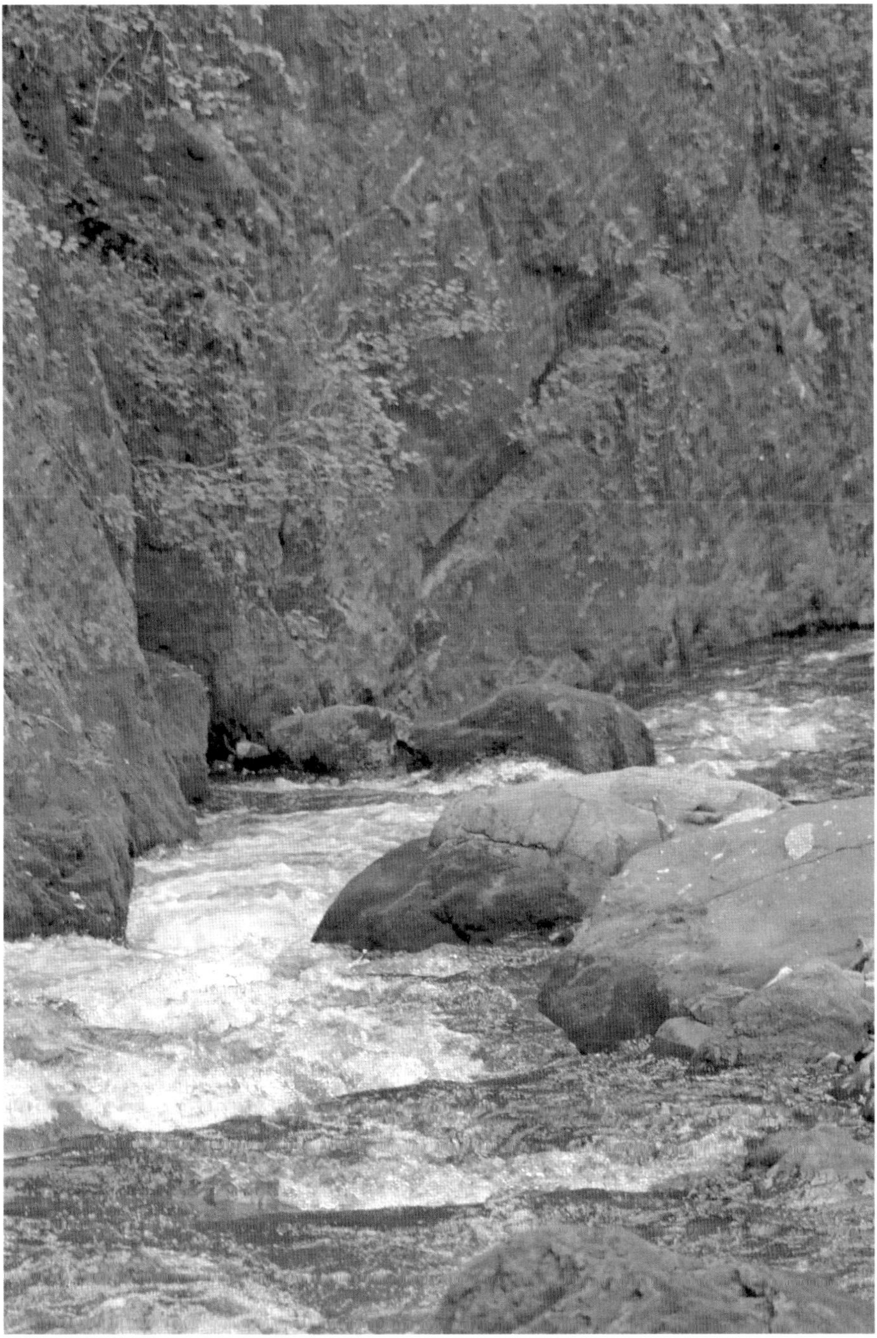

American Fork River moves past the Membrane wall, American Fork Canyon. *Author photo.*

like Adams began cleaning routes (a process that involves knocking off dangerously loose chunks of rock) that these climbs revealed themselves.

This spot, in fact this canyon and so many more, would be undeveloped for sport climbing if it weren't for the introduction of the 1984 battery-powered Bosch hammer drill. (In toying with titles for this book, I suggested "Where there's a Bosch there's a way." I don't think my editor found it nearly as amusing as I did.) While Bosch meant to (and succeeded in) revolutionizing the construction industry with the drill, I'd bet the company had no idea the effect it would have on outdoor recreation.

The cordless hammer drill wasn't the only reason 1984 was notable for Utah sport climbing. It was also the year Pedersen moved back to Utah after a two-year stint in California, where he had grown up. While Pedersen had experimented with climbing before and the sport had gotten under his skin, his return to Utah would also mark the point when he dove into climbing wholeheartedly. Two years later, in January 1986, Pedersen took his tuition and book money and spent it on living in Joshua Tree for a season. Recalling how all the older adults in his life had warned him what a terrible mistake he was making, Pedersen laughed, "They were all completely wrong. It was one of the greatest trips I've ever done." But perhaps the most important event of that trip happened when Bart Doniki mentioned that there were two new climbers burning it up in Utah County: Speed and Phil Cook.

Speed had started climbing only a year earlier, in 1985, when a friend saw him wearing a pair of Patagonia shorts and asked him if he wanted to go climbing. "It was [as] simple as that, serendipity," Speed mentioned to me with a laugh.

Pedersen took note to look up Cook and Speed when he returned home to Utah County. While he hadn't checked American Fork Canyon out yet, Pedersen had been exploring the climbing possibilities of Utah County at large. Most of his time had been spent in Provo, where Rock Canyon had already seen the development of a few dozen traditional routes and some bouldering problems by various students from nearby Brigham Young University. Pedersen had already found several climbing partners in Utah County, including Bill Boyle, the man who would later be referred to as the "invisible army."

Boyle first started climbing while attending Utah State University (USU) in Logan, Utah. A co-worker told him that her husband frequently climbed and was looking for partners. After being introduced, the two climbed some of the older traditional routes in Logan Canyon, like the *Hobbit Hole* and the *Orc Stone*. After graduating from USU, Boyle struggled to find work and briefly found himself in North Carolina, where he continued to climb, but after six to nine months, he moved back to Utah and found a job working with the state Developmental Center. Within a matter of years, the Developmental Center would relocate to American Fork, just minutes away from the mouth of the canyon. Done with school and having found steady work, Boyle had a lot of free time on his hands, allowing him to climb and explore the area at will.

Pedersen himself had first started climbing as a student at BYU in the fall of 1981. Pedersen and dorm mate Bart Dahneke had purchased a bunch of climbing gear and a couple of books and went out to experiment. "We did a lot of self-teaching. That may sound crazy, but we were very careful about it. We tested things close to the ground." This is a characteristic that follows Pedersen to this day. When you talk to climbers about Jeff Pedersen, they note his emphasis on safety and proper technique, an emphasis I experienced myself while taking a class from him at the Quarry rock climbing gym in Provo, Utah, in 2003. Pedersen's first climbing-related memory came earlier, when he was a kid from California living in Utah for the very first time. He hiked Rock Canyon and was walking past the Green Gate area when he saw a wiry little guy with long hair doing a circuit on a portion of rock known as Chicago Overhang. "The guy looked so light and strong, like he was just defying gravity. I'd never seen anything like it," Pedersen recalled. The wiry climber was Mark Ward, an early icon of Utah county climbing.

By the spring of 1986, Pedersen, Boyle and Speed had started climbing together regularly. "We were fast friends immediately," noted Speed, adding, "There were more of us that were really into pushing grades and trying harder climbs. There were four or five or six of us, but a lot of those guys ended up dropping off, getting married and whatnot."

According to Pedersen, one of his first memories of American Fork Canyon was standing at what is now known as the Division Wall and thinking, "Man, this is just hideous," even walking up to the wall and grabbing hold of the loose rock to confirm its rotten nature. "Why can't we have any good climbing here, like Smith Rock [in Colorado]," he recalled thinking. Looking back, Pedersen noted, "We needed to learn that a crowbar and a sledgehammer and a blow tube and a dust broom were part of a route builder's kit in AF [American Fork]. Not to manufacture a route but to remove a death block that might kill someone [when it pulls off]." (I've experienced the dangers of bad rock firsthand while bouldering on some choss in Logan, Utah. An undercling blew off, sending a basketball-size chunk of rock slamming into my face.) Despite their initial hesitations, American Fork Canyon held a world of spectacular climbing behind cobwebs, debris and loose rocks.

During this time, the Utah County climbers were paying attention to the climbing developments on a national level. Pedersen, as with so many climbers, recalls the influence Allen Watts had on the way their group of climbers looked at things. Watts is often credited with developing the first sport climbing route in America, *Watts Tots* (5.12b, FA Allen Watts) at Smith Rock, Colorado. Pedersen summed up the paradigm shift when he said, "Not everything John Bachar [notable American free climber and vocal opponent of rap bolting] said needs to be the law," adding, "And I mean no disrespect to Bachar." The more athletic nature of this new climbing had great appeal for the small group of climbers. This inspired several trips to places like Red Rocks, Las Vegas, with their friend Mike Tupper, who lived in the area. This is one of the first places they experienced/experimented with rap bolting. By 1987, Pedersen and others had begun bolting in Hobble Creak Canyon and a few other obscure Utah County canyons. Boyle would pick up some extra experiences in bolting sport routes with Chris Barnes and Jeff Rhodes just over the Utah/Idaho border at the City of Rocks.

Later in 1988, Pedersen, Boyle and Speed were approached by Steve Gibb, a talented young climber, about a cave (Black Magic) he'd discovered in American Fork Canyon. Speed recalled that Gibb, a high school student from Provo, had been ditching school and hanging out up American Fork Canyon, as he put it, "doing what high school kids do" (though, I imagine that description can create a wide array of images depending on your personal background and high school experience). Gibb and his friends discovered the cave and decided to try to climb it. Afterward, Gibb was quick to encourage Pedersen, Boyle and Speed to check it out. Speed noted, "It's pretty obviously good climbing, you know. Then it started there. Jeff and I went, top-roped it." Borrowing Chris Laycock's drill, the two put the first bolts ever in American Fork Canyon. Over the next year, the trio explored the canyon with greater and greater interest.

According to Speed, "[They'd] tasted the limestone in American Fork just in October of '88, and it started very slowly. Then, basically, it got cold and a lot of things happened during that short period of time." That short period of time Speed refers to was the winter of 1988.

For many climbers, winter is either a downtime or a time for road trips to warmer locations, like southern Utah or Red Rocks. Regardless of how climbers deal with winter falling all over their local crags, it provides the same opportunity: a chance for reflection, be it conscious or subconscious. I'd imagine the experiences the three climbers had shared that fall in American Fork Canyon, limited as they were, sat in their minds, taunting them. The

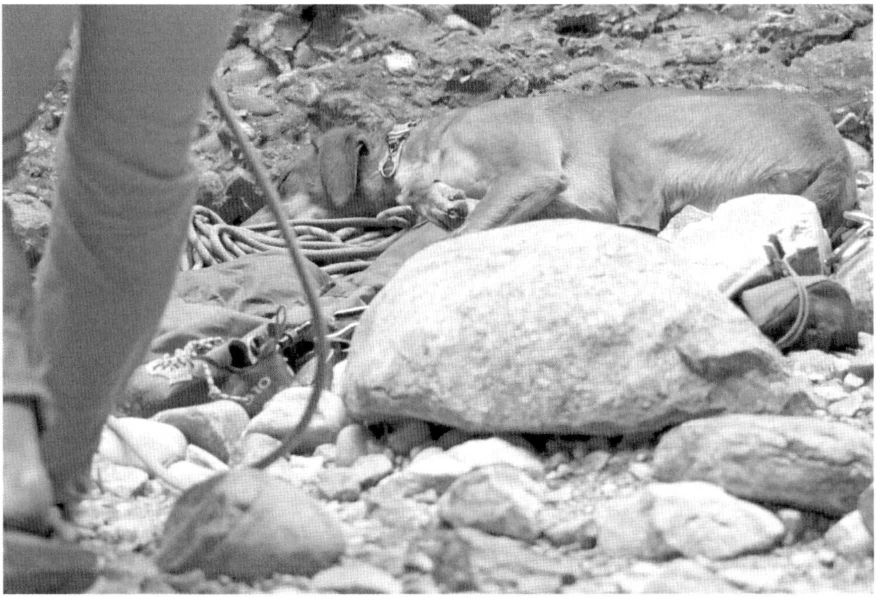

A crag dog takes a nap. *Author photo.*

winter months weren't a waste, however. Santa—or, rather, Mr. and Mrs. Speed—would make a purchase that proved to be an essential part of that firestorm of development that came with the spring. Speed had asked for a Bosch cordless power drill for Christmas. When I try to picture myself in his place, approaching my parents to tell them that I wanted a drill for Christmas so that I could place bolts twenty, thirty and forty feet up a cliff, I don't see it going over as smoothly as it must have for Speed.

Recalling the role that winter played in the trio's progression into route development in American Fork Canyon, Speed said:

> *We started in Red Rocks and bolted some routes down there, like* The Gallery *for instance. Once the snow cleared in February, I went back up American Fork Canyon—I worked at a foundry near there—and I started, in February of '89, I put up a couple of routes, and then Bill* [Boyle] *and Jeff* [Pedersen] *came up and climbed them with me, and it just started a firestorm. And then Bill, within like two months, had hiked the entire canyon. And probably by himself had put in a hundred bolts on five different cliffs, and he would literally, in like a weekend, develop an entire wall. Like, Cannabis Wall was developed in one weekend, and the Red Corners was developed over a couple of weekends. The Billboard was a*

climbing area over the course of like two weekends. Things like that, the campgrounds, everything just happened really quickly.

That spring of 1989 saw the development of over one hundred routes in American Fork Canyon, an unheard-of level of development, especially coming from three people.

Pedersen remembered how the three men would use their climbing rest days to explore the canyon, "like kids in a candy store." Unlike today, when most people first experience climbing as youths or teens under parental supervision, the trio and the friends they climbed with were adults. They had jobs and pressure from society to behave a certain way. When Pedersen told his father that he wasn't going to apply to graduate schools because he wanted to be a climber instead, his father responded by asking, "How much money does that pay?" While Pedersen has clearly turned climbing into a living now, at the time, the decision put some strain on that relationship; they are able to laugh about it now.

The group became so focused on pushing limits, not of safety but of athleticism and difficulty, that everything else fell away. Their focus and drive to both climb and find newer and more challenging climbs seems to have fueled the group in a way few people ever experience.

Speaking about the level of the group's motivation, Speed noted, "Other things in life take a backseat. You know, all of us were only focused on climbing. The three of us especially, and that's why we stayed doing it. It was partially selfish, I guess." He added, "And then work, I made enough money to survive and that's it. That's all I cared about....So, it was just about climbing. Everything else faded. I'd blow off work. Cheat work as much as I could." Their focus and passion payed off. American Fork Canyon yielded some of, if not *the*, most challenging routes in the world at the time. By 1990, the ignored canyon filled with loose limestone had become the focus of American climbing for a period and would host many of the country's best climbers. Scott Frye, Dale Goddard and others temporarily took up residence in the canyon. Even foreign climbers like Australian Geoff Weigand called the canyon home for a time.

Fueling that fire behind climbing in American Fork Canyon was the visit of a few notable French climbers. Snowbird ski resort in Salt Lake City had hosted the first ever World Cup of Climbing in June 1988, and word of climbing in Utah began to spread internationally. Later, after development in American Fork Canyon had started, French superstar climbers Didier Raboutou and Jibe Tribout paid a visit to Utah and were told to check out the newly discovered limestone canyon. "We freaked," said Speed of meeting Raboutou and Tribout, two of the best climbers in the world at the time. "I mean, we had only heard about these guys in magazines, and the only reason they were in Utah was because of the climbing competition at Snowbird. And they freaked out; they loved it…not only enjoying it, but raving about the quality and how interesting it was." Pedersen noted that the approval of the French climbers added a lot of validity to what they had done.

The climbs in American Fork Canyon and the techniques used to develop them—cleaning off sections of loose, dangerous rock while on rappel, bringing in ladders and crowbars—affected the trajectory of sport climbing as a whole. "The Hell Cave is arguably the highest concentration of the steepest routes in the world at the time," said Speed. "It was steeper than Volx. It was steeper than anything in Germany. There was nothing like it. And if there hadn't have been ladders involved in bolting it, ladders and automatic drills, the crag wouldn't have existed. And so I think a lot of people came and looked at what we had done in Hell [Cave] and went home and said, 'Oh, we can do the same thing here.' I mean, I think the French went back home and it even influenced them to develop steeper and steeper walls there." Speed added, "It played at least a small role in opening peoples' eyes to new possibilities."

The amount of attention sport climbing brought to the canyon could have caused conflict with local land managers, but because Pedersen, Speed and Boyle had done such a good job of establishing a relationship with them—Pedersen recalled volunteering for every trail crew he could to help show that they wanted to take care of the canyon—no conflict ever arose. The trio's approach to working with American Fork Canyon's land managers could have saved developers in other areas a lot of grief and aided in other canyons' development.

Likewise, there was no ethics conflict between climbers over bolting methods as there had been and would be elsewhere. "We worked with what we had, so for me, I didn't really think about that stuff," said Speed.

> *We did what we thought was right, and we tried to keep it as pure and natural as possible. We were looking for the hardest things Mother Nature could provide. That was it, just the hardest physical challenge and looking to climb the impossible. That was the goal. That was my goal. Bill Boyle's goal was maybe different. You could talk to him about that. And Jeff Pedersen's goal was maybe different, but my goal was to find the hardest,*

> *craziest, most difficult thing that Mother Nature could provide. And what I mean by Mother Nature is the most natural climbing experience possible in a place where you still have to glue holds and it's funky, you know.*

As they were the first to climb in American Fork Canyon, there was nobody to tell them that they were doing things the wrong way. They were able to take what they'd learned at Smith Rock and Red Rocks and get creative, evolve it to work with the steep and often loose limestone of American Fork Canyon.

Getting the history of American Fork Canyon's sport climbing right has proven tricky. When Drew Bedford wrote the first climbing article on the canyon, there was a scramble for people to get their pictures taken on certain routes. Pedersen didn't feel a need to get his photo taken. As an unfortunate result, the article inadvertantly made it look as if only two people had developed the canyon. As time passed and people asked who'd developed Pedersen's routes, the joke answer became "the invisible man." The joke would grow when Randy Leavitt wrote an article on Pedersen for *Rock and Ice* where he referred to him as the invisible man. Then, highlighting the absurd amount of routes put up by Boyle, Leavitt added that Boyle must be the invisible army.

But the story of sport climbing in American Fork Canyon isn't the story of one man or two or even, as much as it could be, the story of three. At its core, the story is about having passion fuel your hunt for what you want so that you can see it where others might not, where only the possibility of it actually exists. Who knows how long the limestone of American Fork Canyon would have gone undeveloped if Boyle, Speed and Pedersen hadn't been so desperate to feed their hunger for climbing. But they were, and they had the ingenuity to build on what others had done and solve the unique problems that stood in the way of what they were hunting.

5
LOGAN CANYON

For almost ten years, I frequented the dolomite cliff bands of Logan Canyon. I came to the cliffs for a mix of vertical exploration and personal introspection. These limestone walls are home to hundreds of sport climbing routes. I looked at each one the same way my mom looks at a Sudoku puzzle. But these cliffs are home to more than the climbing antics of college kids. Poking out proudly from the corner of a dolomite outcropping, grown from a nestling bed of moss, is the Maguire primrose. Its thin stem, one green swipe of an artist brush, leads to five reddish-lavender petals. This flower is a survivor of the rarest kind. The Maguire primrose became federally protected on August 21, 1985, when it was listed as a threatened species. According to the Maguire Primrose Recovery Plan (MPRP), the flower grows only in the lower elevations of Logan Canyon. You could travel the world—France, Italy, Africa, China, you could see all that those lands hold—but if you want to see the Maguire primrose, you'll have to travel through miles of cow grazing pasture into the corner of Cache County, Utah. In fact, the total number of Maguire primroses is estimated around three thousand individual flowers.

The first section of Logan Canyon rock to have any form of climbing bolt in it is found just outside what is now called the China Wall Cave. The route, known as *The Bolt Ladder*, was most likely created as a tool to practice placing gear for aid climbing. In trying to discover who may have established it, I found the same answer over and over again: "I doubt anybody knows that at this point." And that is one of the driving forces behind this book.

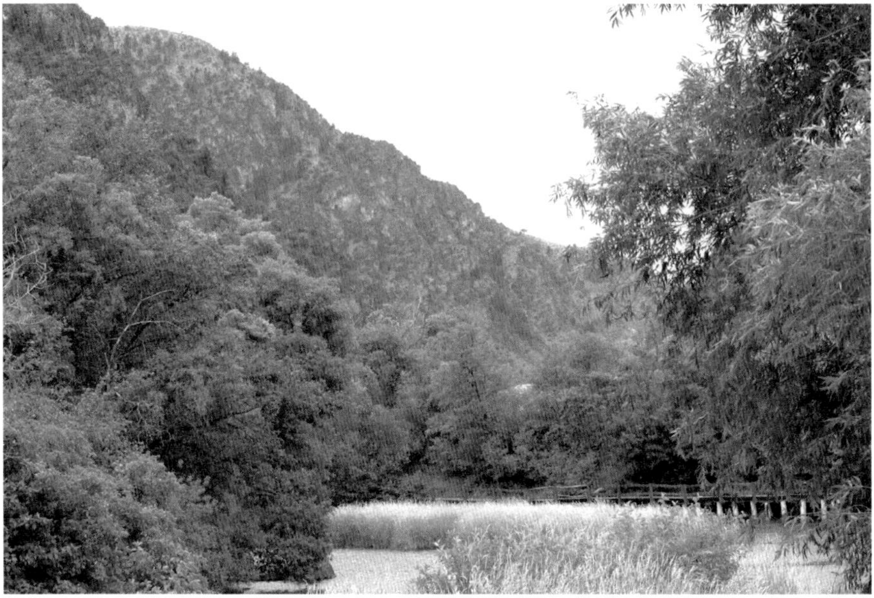

A bridge crosses the Logan River in Logan Canyon. *Author photo.*

While the names of climbers who claimed many (certainly not all) of the first ascents for sport climbs in Utah are recorded, if something of the history surrounding those names isn't recorded, they will turn into nothing more than cold facts. The history will die, and when someone asks how sport climbing in Logan Canyon, or Maple Canyon, Moab or Ibex started, the only answer they'll find will be: "I doubt anybody knows that at this point."

When I think of climbing in Logan Canyon, the first name that comes to mind is Bill Boyle. One member of the American Fork Canyon trinity (with Jeff Pedersen and Boone Speed), Boyle actually started climbing in Logan Canyon. After the eruption of sport climbing that took place in American Fork in 1992, an eruption that thrust American Fork Canyon (and Utah sport climbing) onto the world's map, Boyle eventually returned to Logan Canyon and bolted an absurd number of solid sport routes. But Boyle wasn't the start of sport climbing in Logan Canyon. That mark on history belongs to another group of climbers.

In 1990, Matt Cupal moved from Wyoming, where he had been an active trad climber, to Logan, Utah. According to Cupal, there wasn't a climbing shop or gym at the time (Logan's trademark gear shop, the Trailhead, didn't exist yet), and there didn't seem to be much of a climbing community (though, several climbers were out exploring the canyon's limestone faces

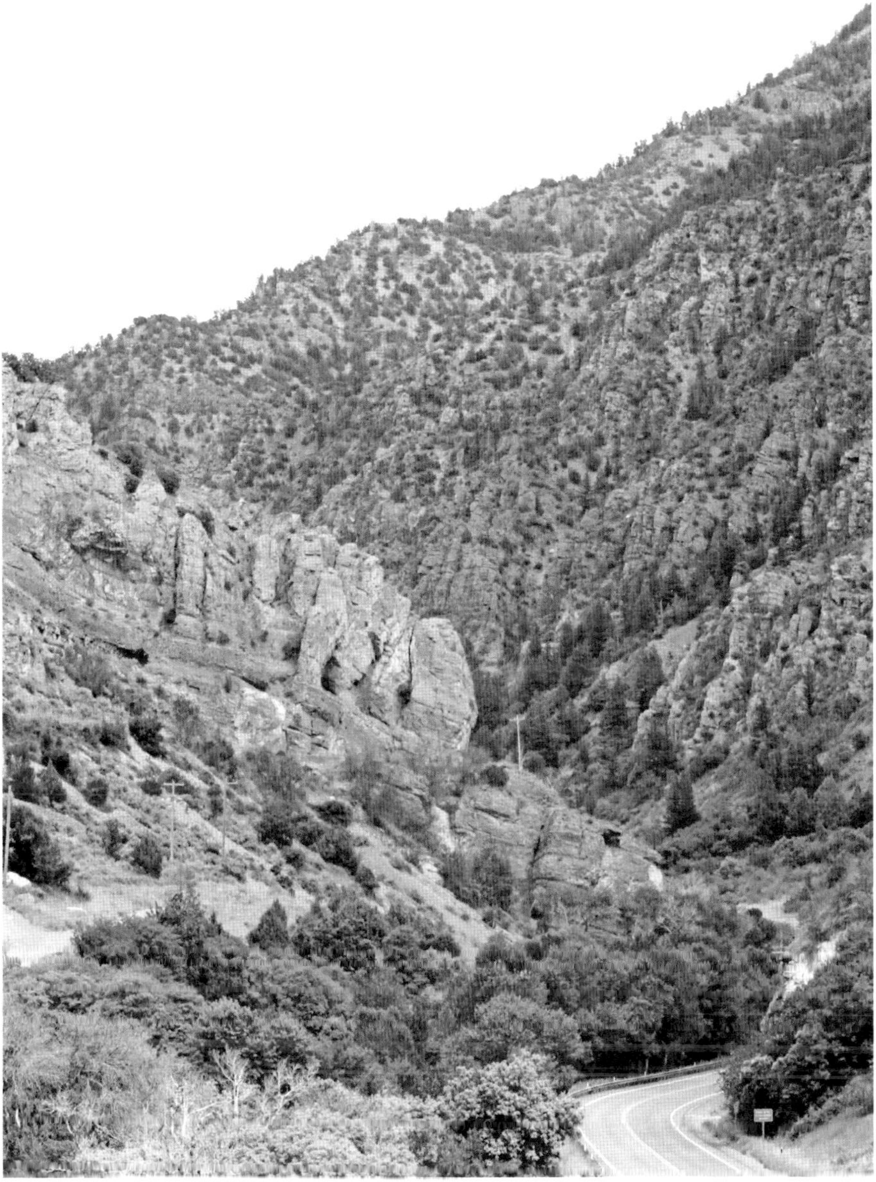

An image of Logan Canyon as seen from the entrance, Logan, Utah. *Author photo.*

and pinnacles). It was by chance that Cupal saw two climbers on the Bolt Ladder one day. Pulling off to the side of the road, he asked if he could join them. They consented, and the group spent the day climbing together.

This is not an uncommon thing to have happen in Logan Canyon. Well, at the time I'm sure it was, but now, with the spread of sport climbing, the way U.S. Highway 89 has grown into a major byway and the number of Logan Canyon crags that are visible from the road, it seems fairly common for locals to be approached by climbers who are just passing through, see them and decide to stop and do some climbing. The only place I've ever had something like that happen is Logan Canyon, and it seemed to happen to me at least once a year. Much like the pair whom Cupal met, we were always more than happy to have them join us for the day.

Cupal quickly met more climbers, like Logan Canyon mainstays Jim Sherner, Tim Monsell (the author of *Logan Canyon Climbs*, the area's first guidebook, which I still own a beat-to-hell copy of) and Bob Sinclair, who would teach Cupal how to bolt. Slowly, these men and others began to establish sport climbing areas in Logan Canyon. At first, these crags were close to the road, areas like Fucoidal Quartzite and 385, areas that, because of their ease of access, are now overrun on weekends and at least busy on any day with good weather.

According to Cupal, the first real sport route bolted in Logan Canyon was most likely a 5.12 established by Bob Sinclair in an area across from First Practice wall—a band of limestone with several enjoyable beginner-grade sport routes that are all able to be set up on top rope if desired. The area across from First Practice wall that bore Sinclair's route has long since been closed due to the presence of the Maguire primrose.

When these first-route developers started working in Logan Canyon, there was no concern regarding the Maguire primrose—not that they were callous in bolting routes near the threatened flower, they just didn't know about it.

What does seem somewhat callous is the way nature and evolution have treated the Maguire primrose. It seems that this universe, which pressed the Maguire primrose into creation from a limestone crack, couldn't care less if the little flower lives or dies. Its stem, a chlorophyll needle, is a thin lifeline between the effervescent flower and the rock it draws its life from. As the MPRP notes, the Maguire primrose is "dependent on the favorable temperature and moisture conditions of its microhabitat…and magnesium carbonates of its soil substrate." The MPRP goes on to say that attempts to transplant the flower to gardens in the valley just a few miles below have been unsuccessful. This world cared enough for beauty to create the

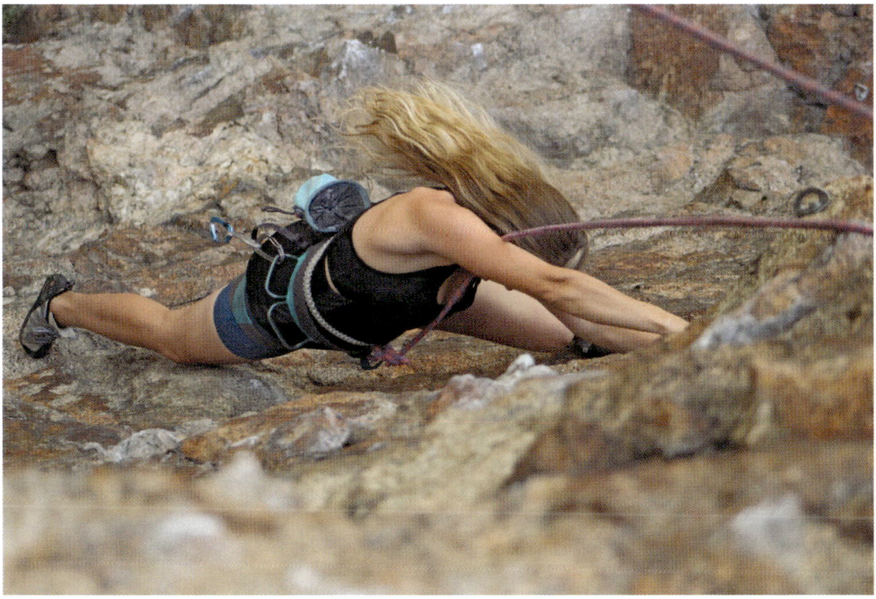

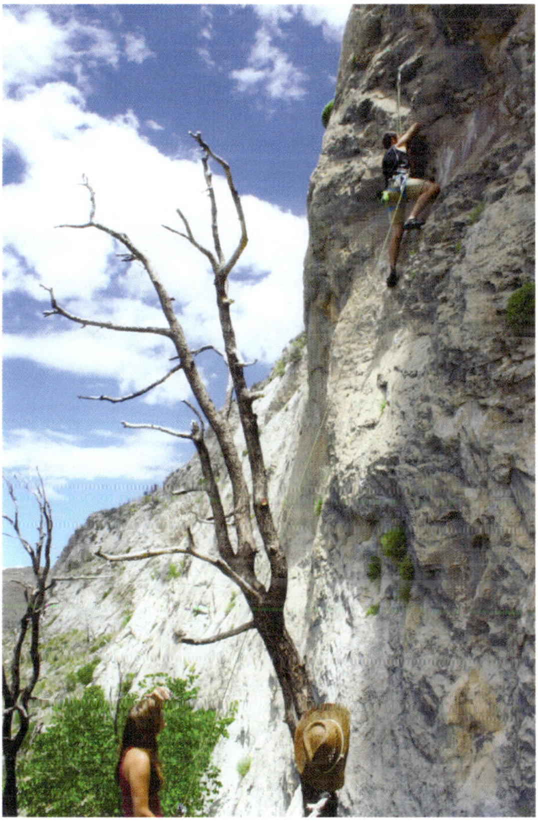

Above: A local climber top-ropes a route at the Ninth Street Crag. *Author photo.*

Left: Christopher Kilburn leads a route out at the Utah Hills in southern Utah. *Author photo.*

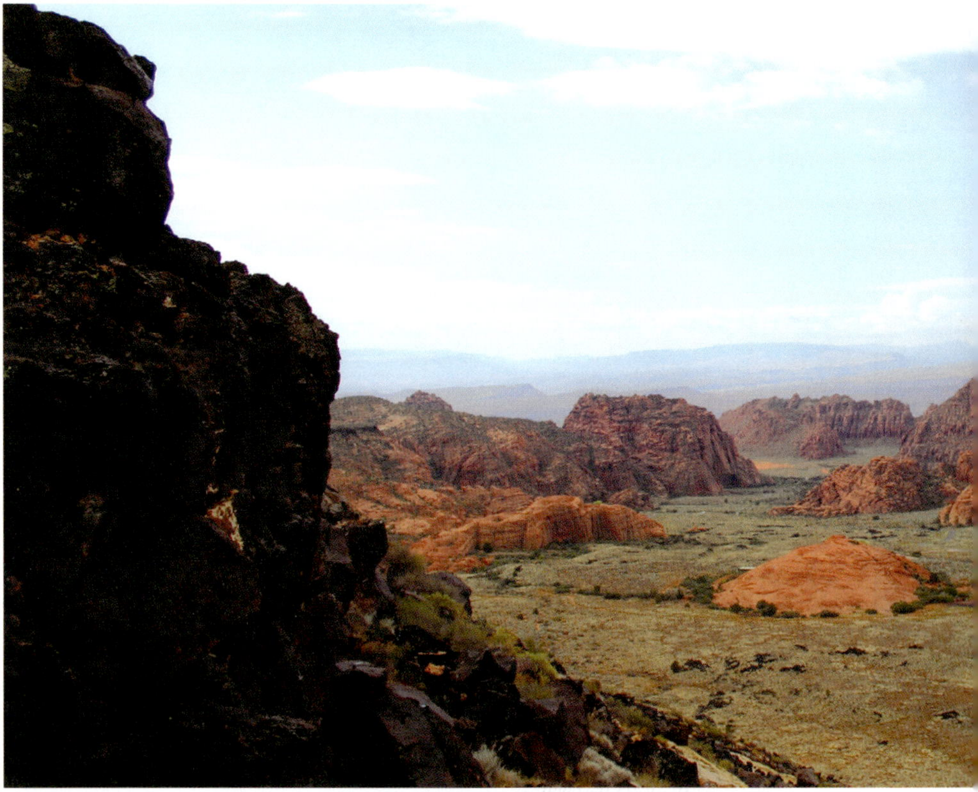

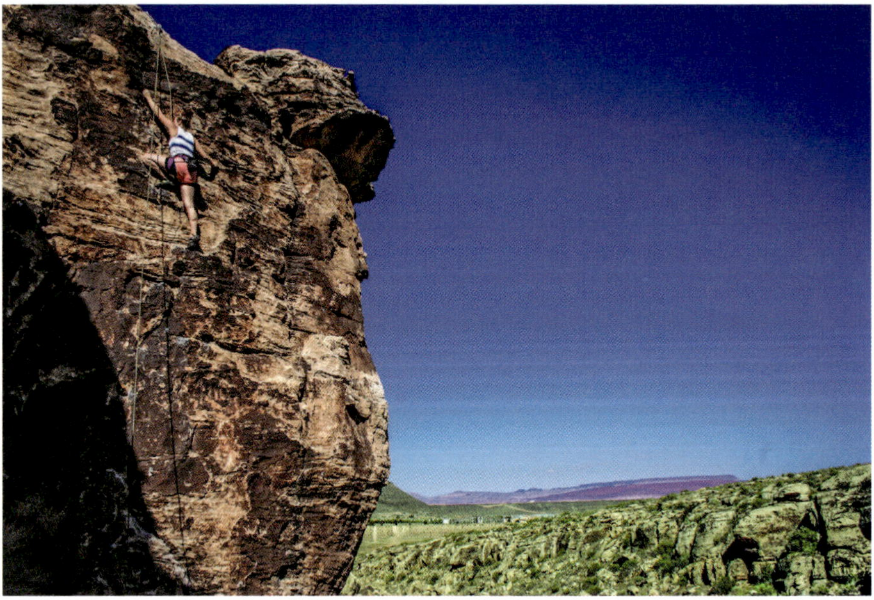

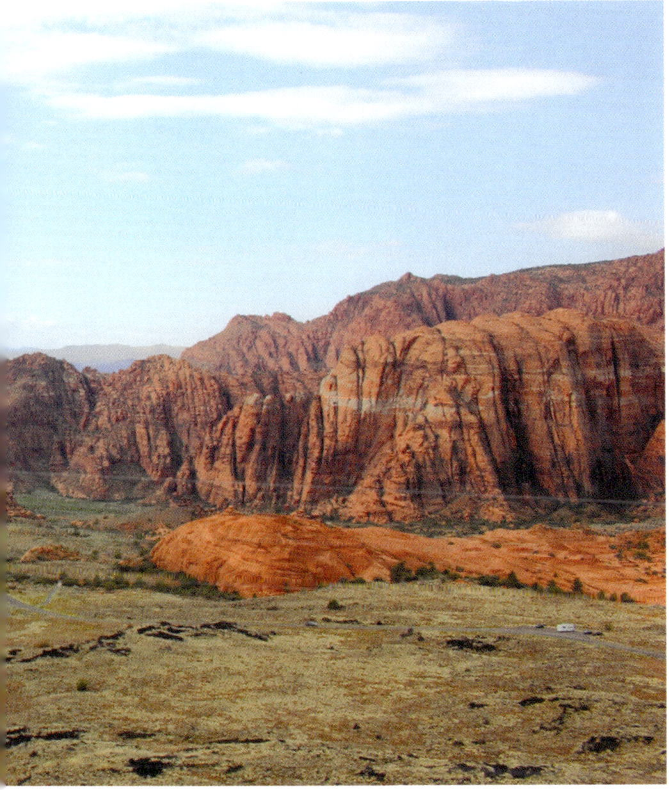

Left: A panorama of Snow Canyon State Park, Utah. *Author photo.*

Opposite, bottom: Lauren Jo Sypniewski top-ropes a route at the Green Valley Gap in southern Utah. *Author photo.*

Below: Picture from below an arch in Moab, Utah, *Photo by and courtesy of Travis Higley*.

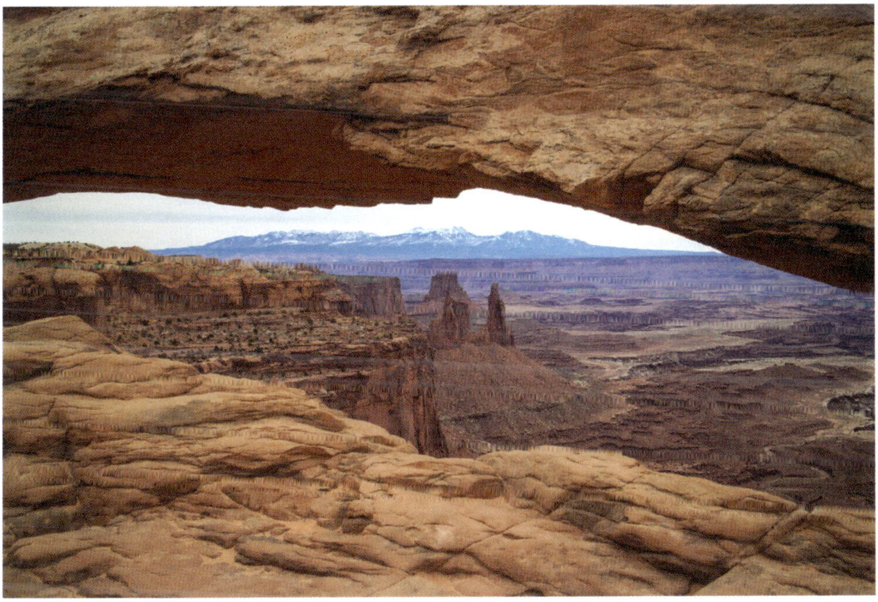

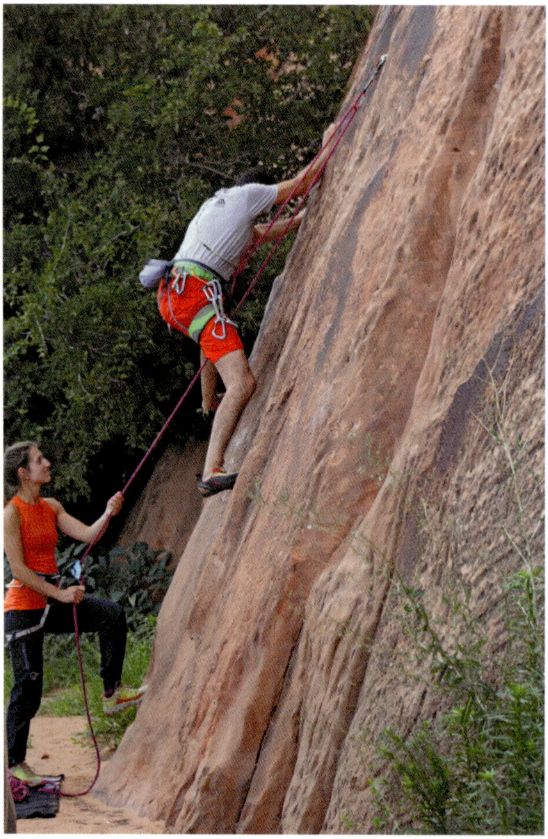

Left: Silvia Di Giorgio and Andrea Carlet on their honeymoon at the Wall Street Crag on Potash Road, Moab, Utah. *Author photo.*

Below: Horizon with an arch in Moab, Utah, *Photo by and courtesy of Travis Higley*.

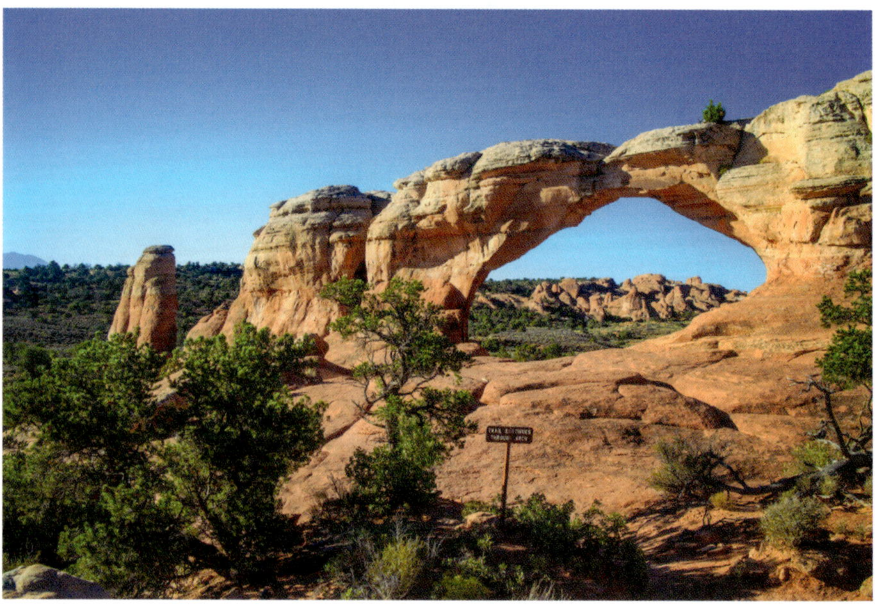

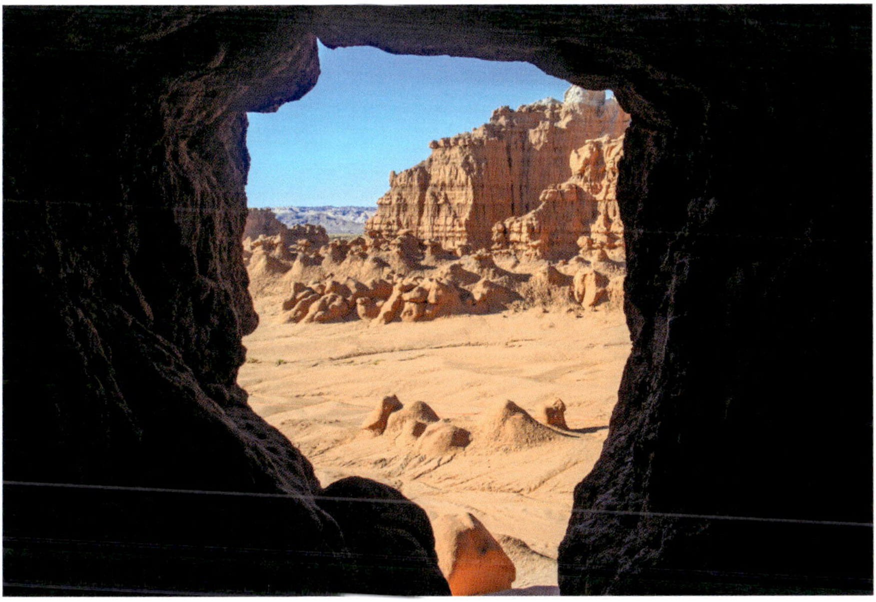

Above: Peeking out from a hole in Moab, Utah, *Photo by and courtesy of Travis Higley.*

Right: Big Cottonwood Creek, Salt Lake City, Utah. *Author photo.*

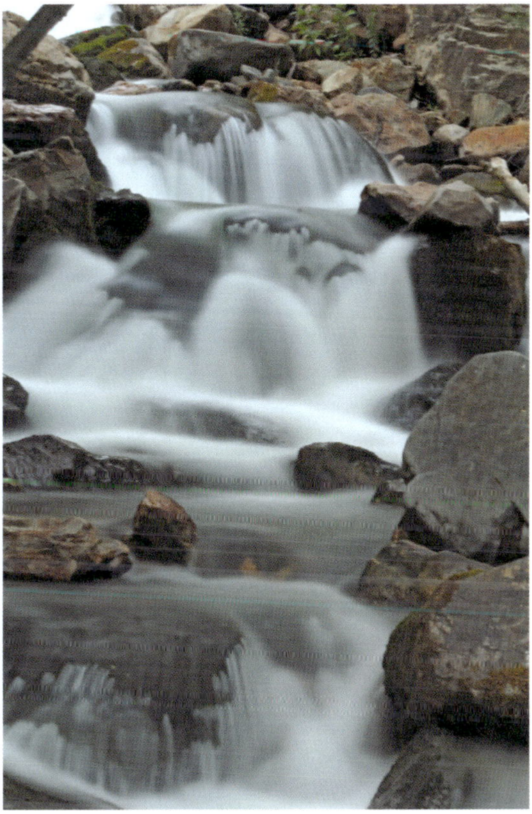

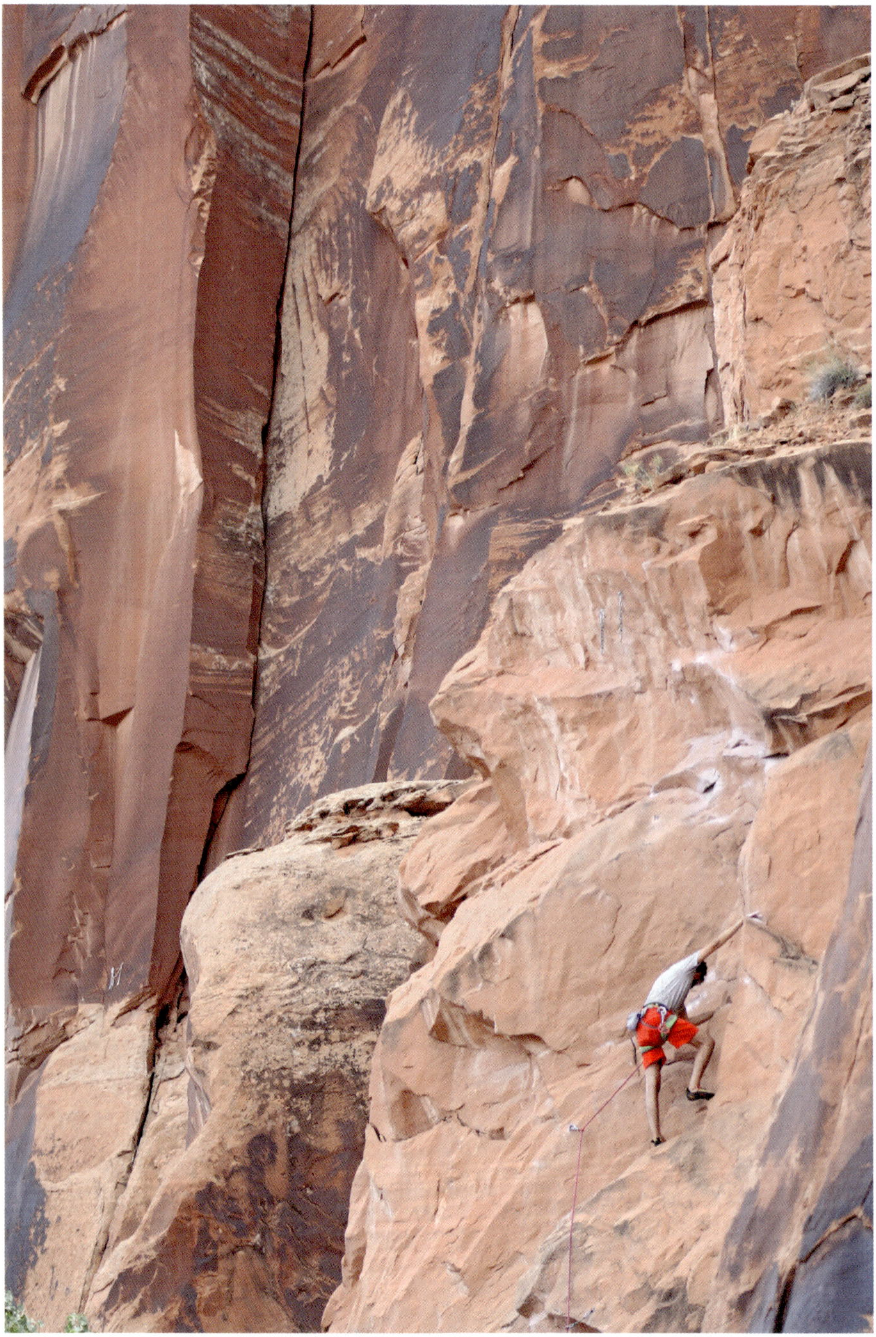

Andrea Carlet leads a climb at the Wall Street Crag on Potash Road, Moab, Utah. *Author photo.*

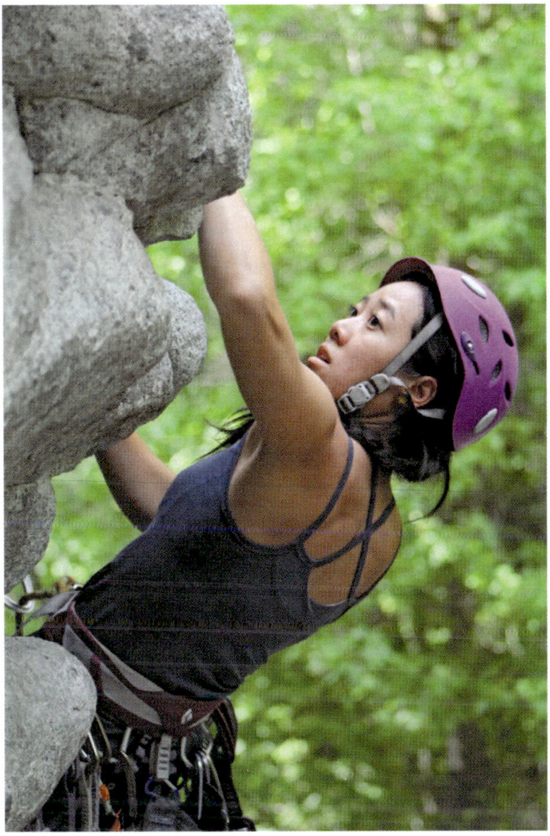

Right: Fok Vuw Chan on *Nuptial Vow* in Ferguson Canyon, Salt Lake City, Utah. *Author photo.*

Below: A snake visits me mid–photo shoot, Ferguson Canyon, Salt Lake City, Utah. *Author photo.*

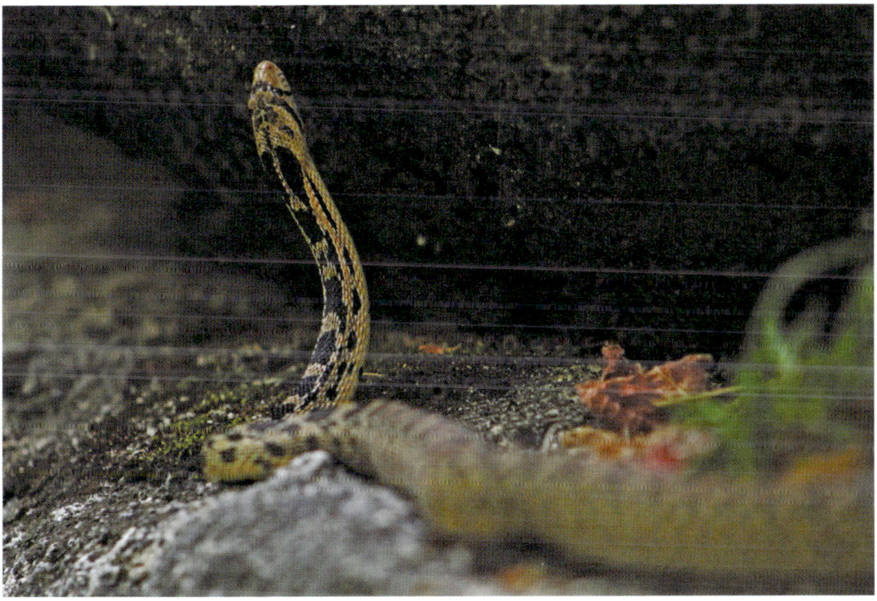

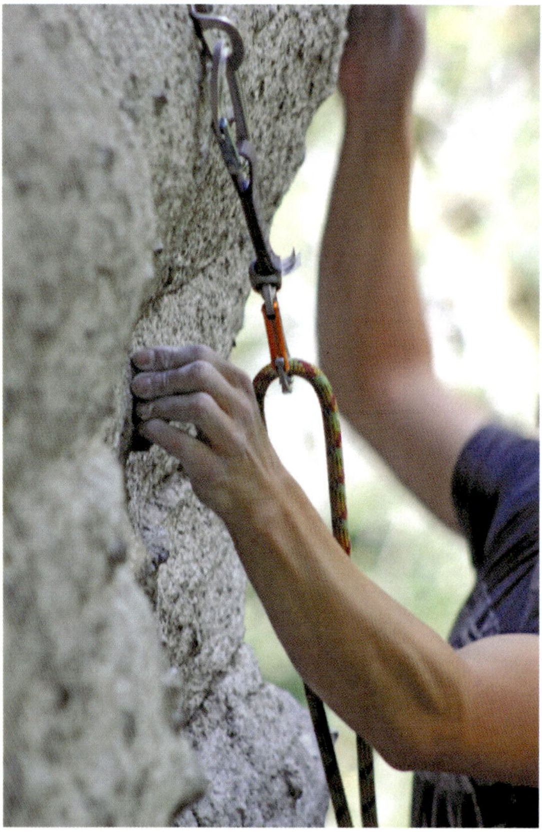

Left: A close-up of a crimp, Ferguson Canyon, Salt Lake City, Utah. *Author photo.*

Below: Big Cottonwood Creek, Salt Lake City, Utah. *Author photo.*

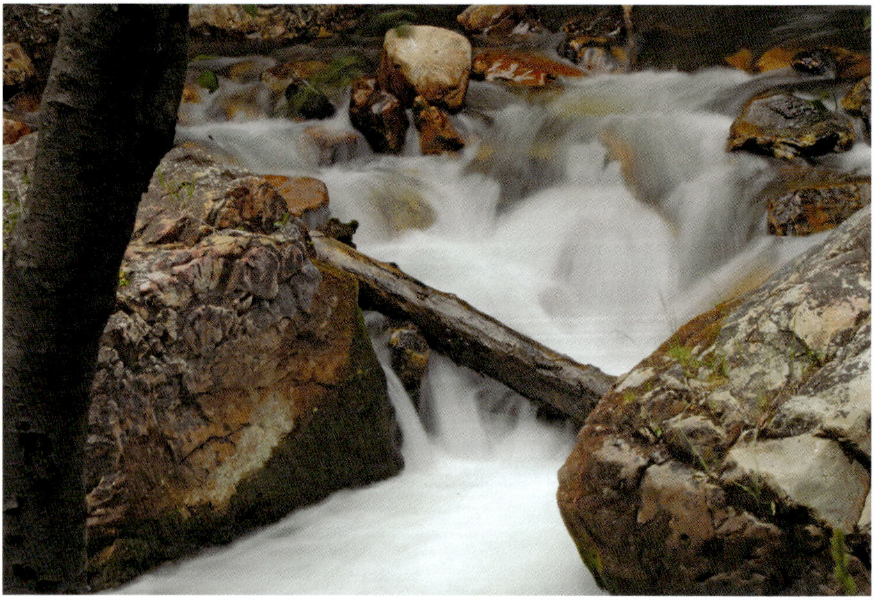

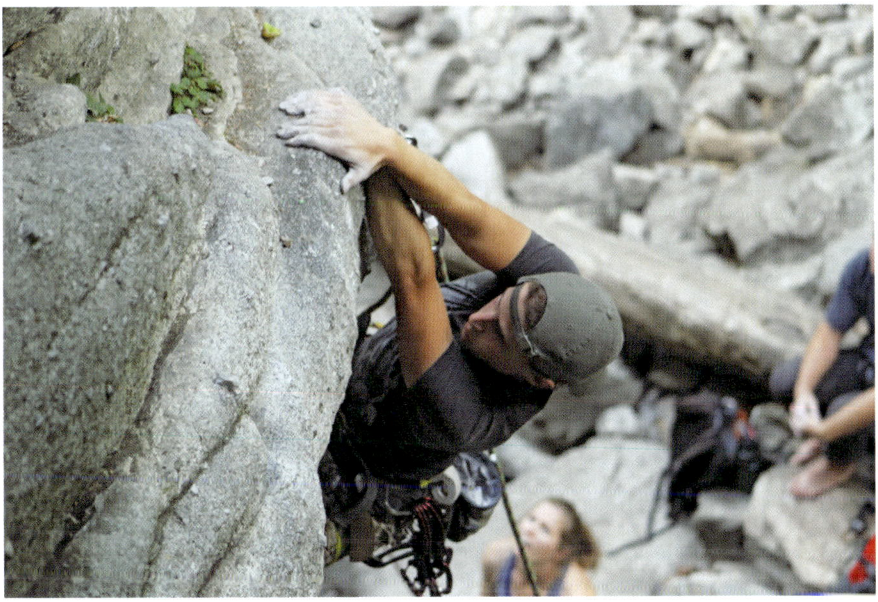

Erik Dutzman on *Monogamy* in Ferguson Canyon, Salt Lake City, Utah. *Author photo.*

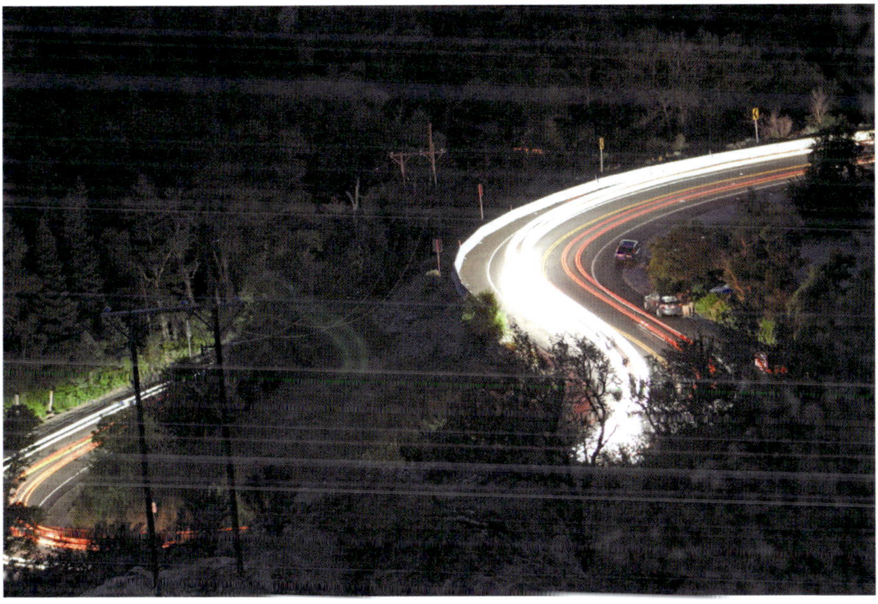

S-bend by night, Big Cottonwood Canyon, Salt Lake City, Utah. *Author photo.*

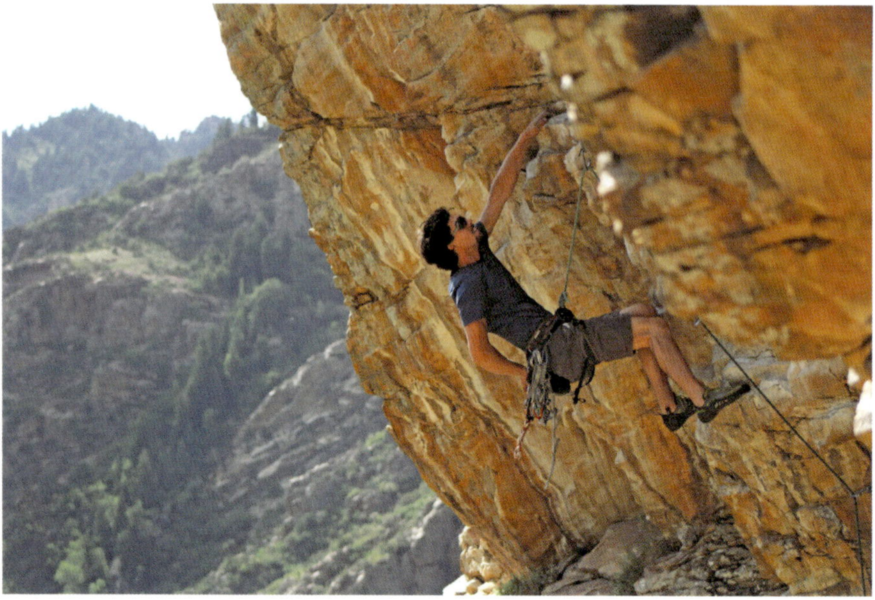

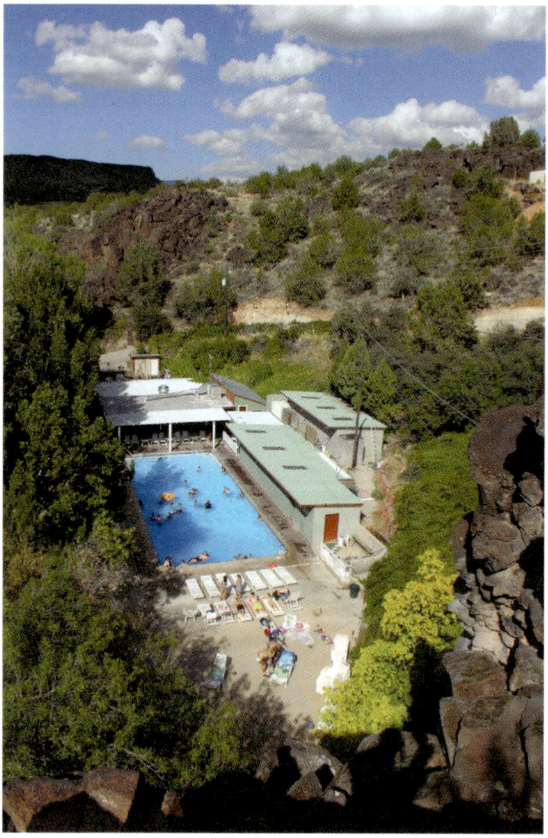

Above: Kailen Fernandez leads on *Black Monday* at the S-bend crag, Big Cottonwood Canyon, Salt Lake City, Utah. *Author photo.*

Left: Veyo Pool from above Crawdad Canyon. *Author photo.*

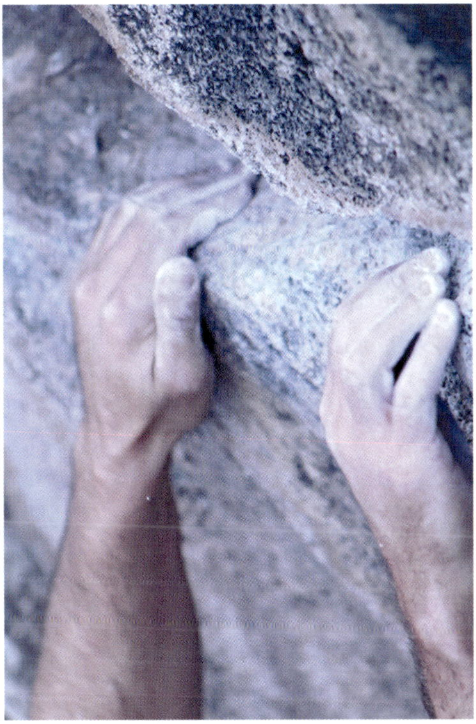

Chalked hands on basalt, Crawdad Canyon. *Author photo.*

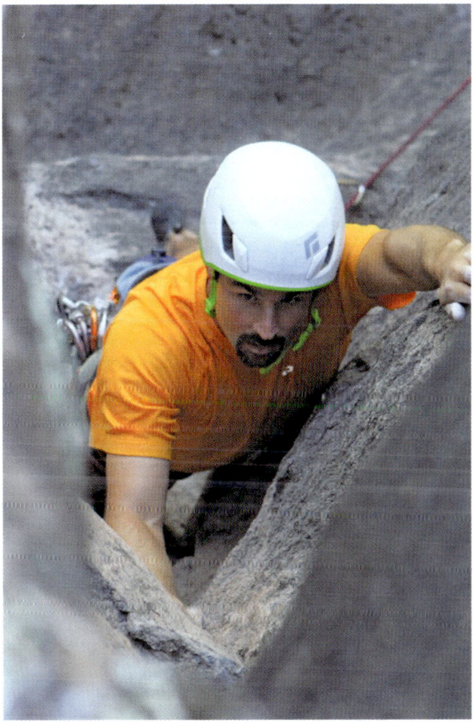

A local climber leads a route in Crawdad Canyon. *Author photo.*

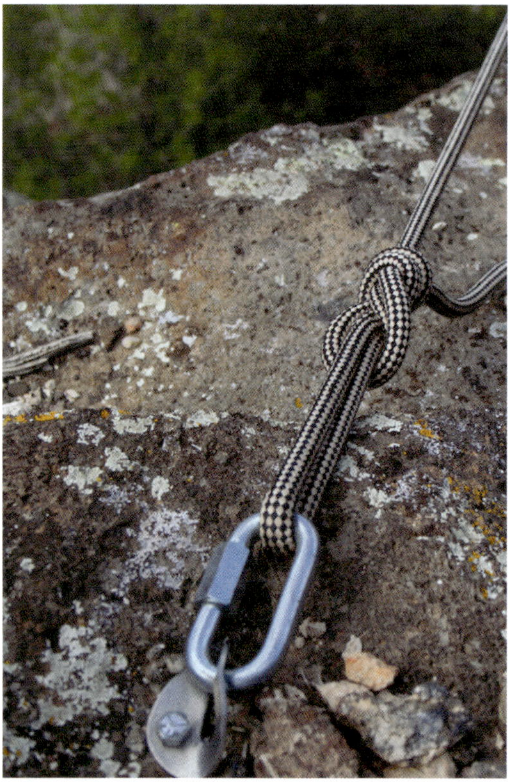

Left: Gear atop Crawdad Canyon. *Author photo.*

Below, left: Shaneen Docton on *Steel Monkey* at the Membrane Wall, American Fork Canyon. *Author photo.*

Below, right: Saloni Shah on *License to Thrill* at the Membrane Wall, American Fork Canyon. *Author photo.*

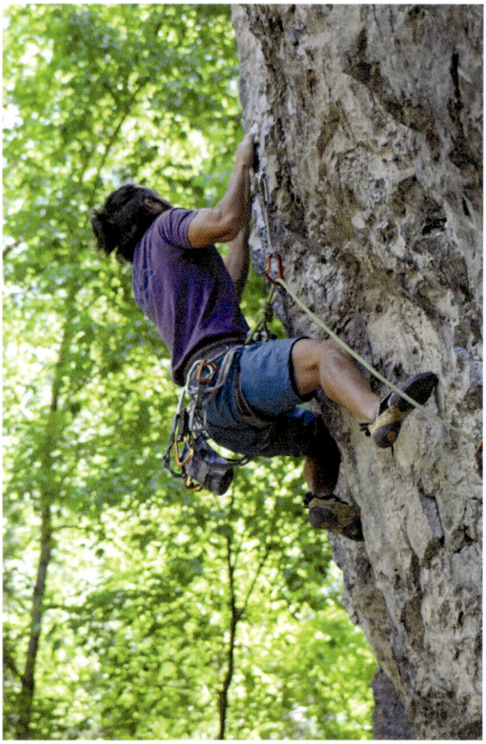

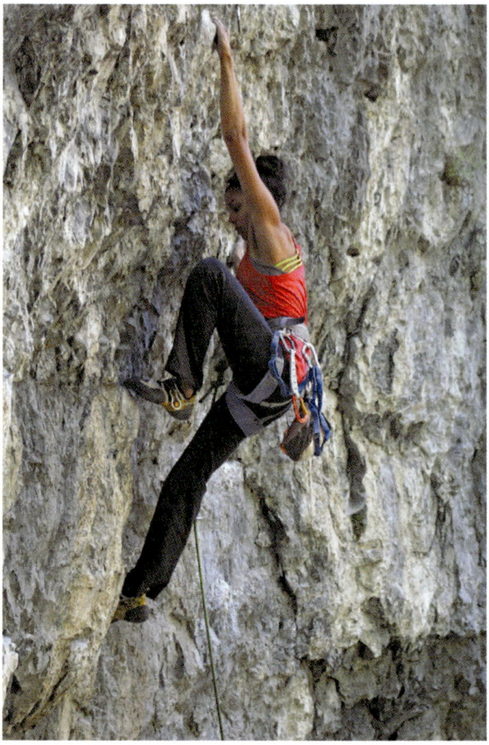

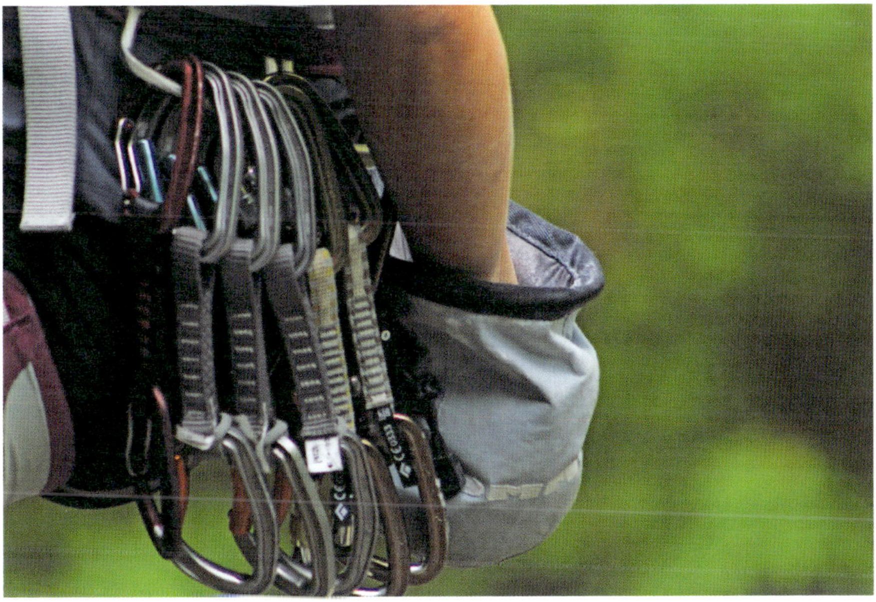

A climber chalks up mid-climb. *Author photo.*

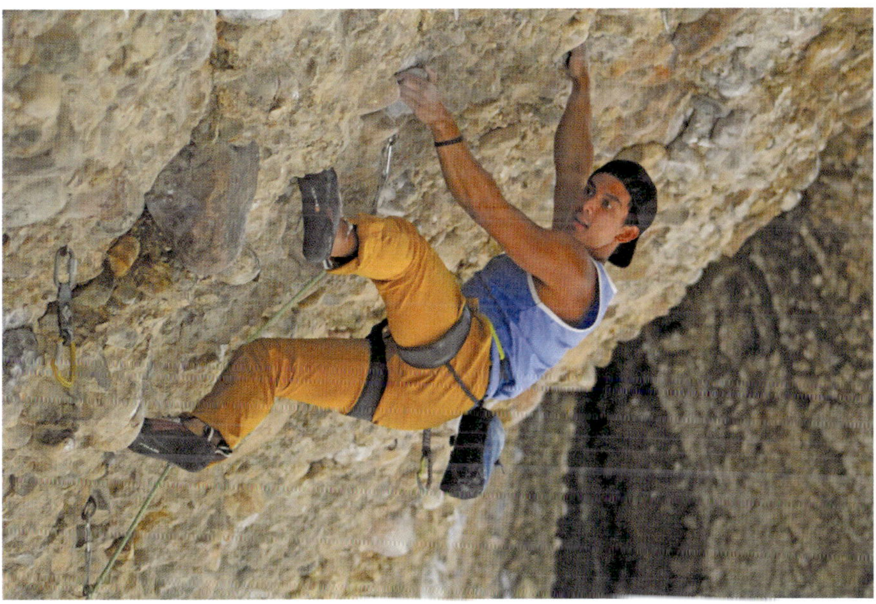

Metro Asunción on Ammo Dump in the Box Canyon at Maple Canyon. *Author photo.*

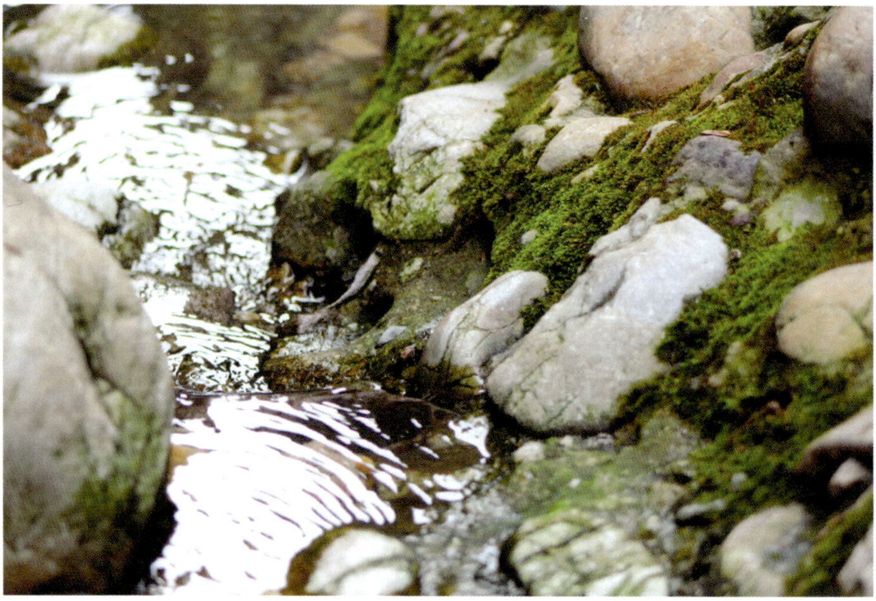

A puddle in Box Canyon at Maple Canyon. *Author photo.*

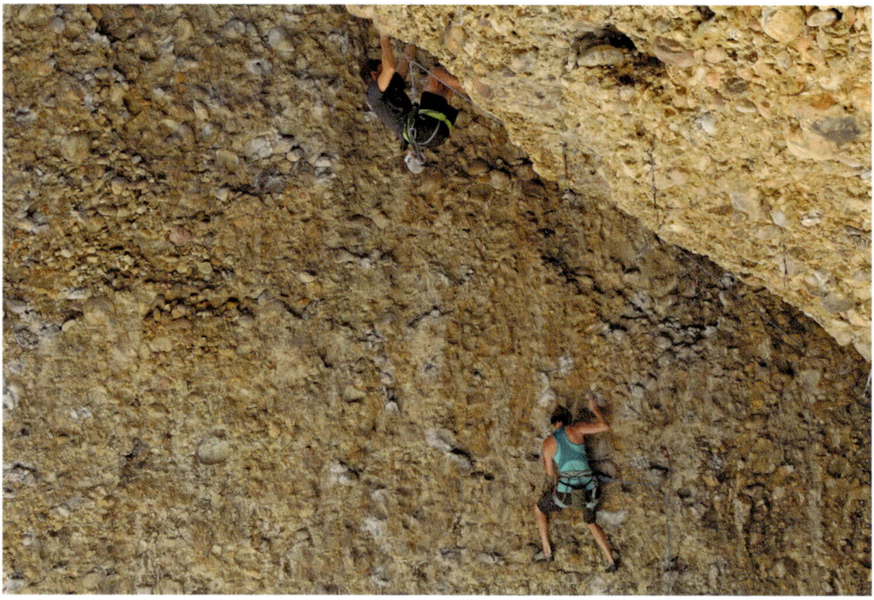

Heath Christensen and Megan Tierney share a wall in the Box Canyon at Maple Canyon. *Author photo.*

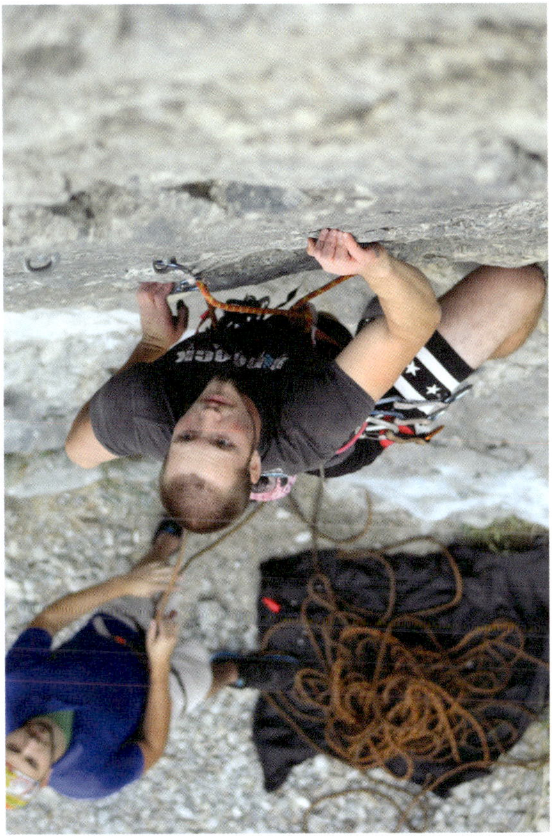

Right: Sean Carter on a roadside route in Logan Canyon. *Author photo.*

Below: Logan Canyon by night. *Author photo.*

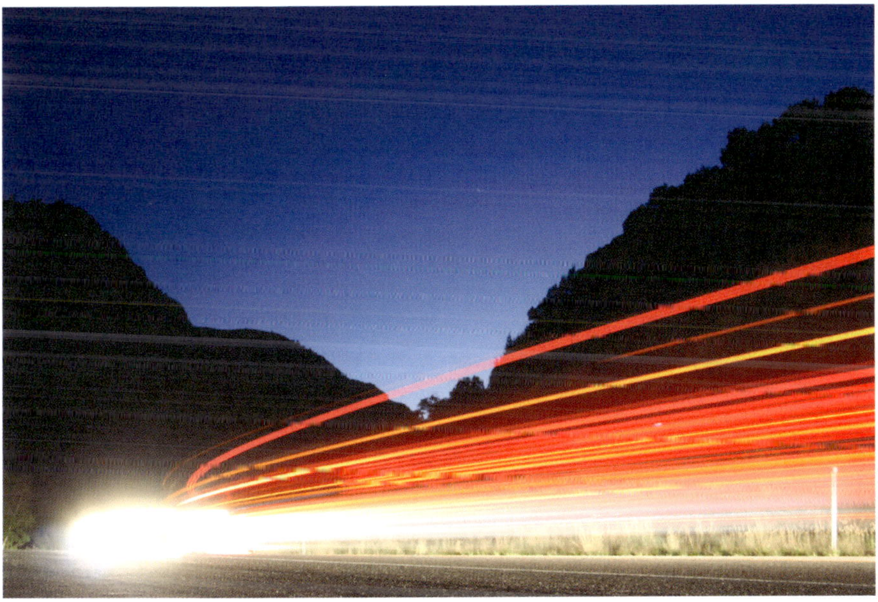

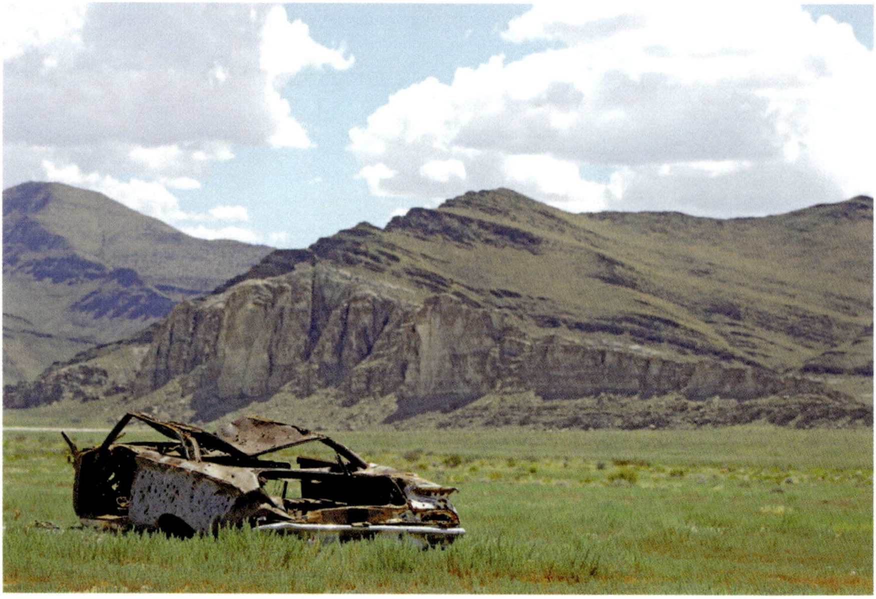

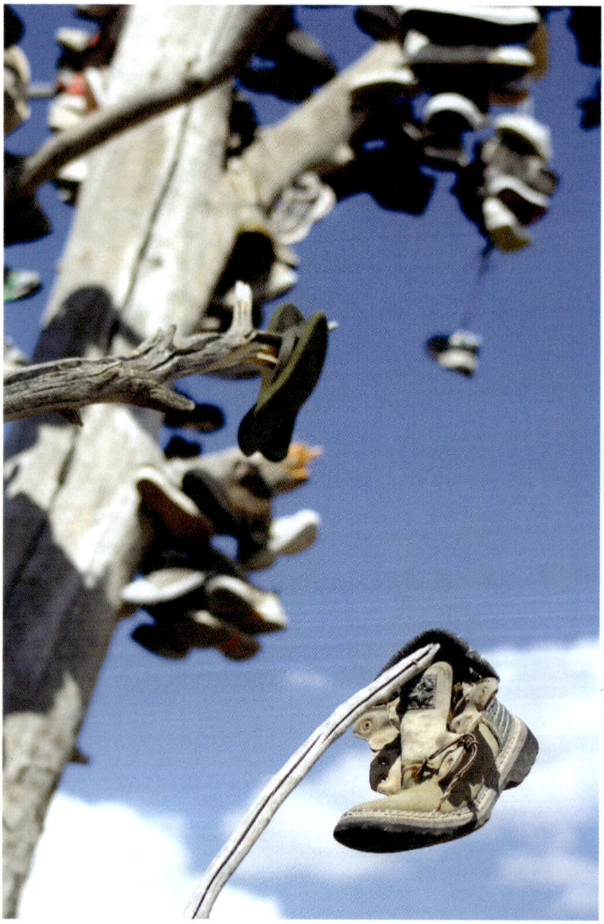

Above: Ibex from a distance. *Author photo.*

Left: Shoe Tree en route from Delta, Utah, to the West Desert. *Author photo.*

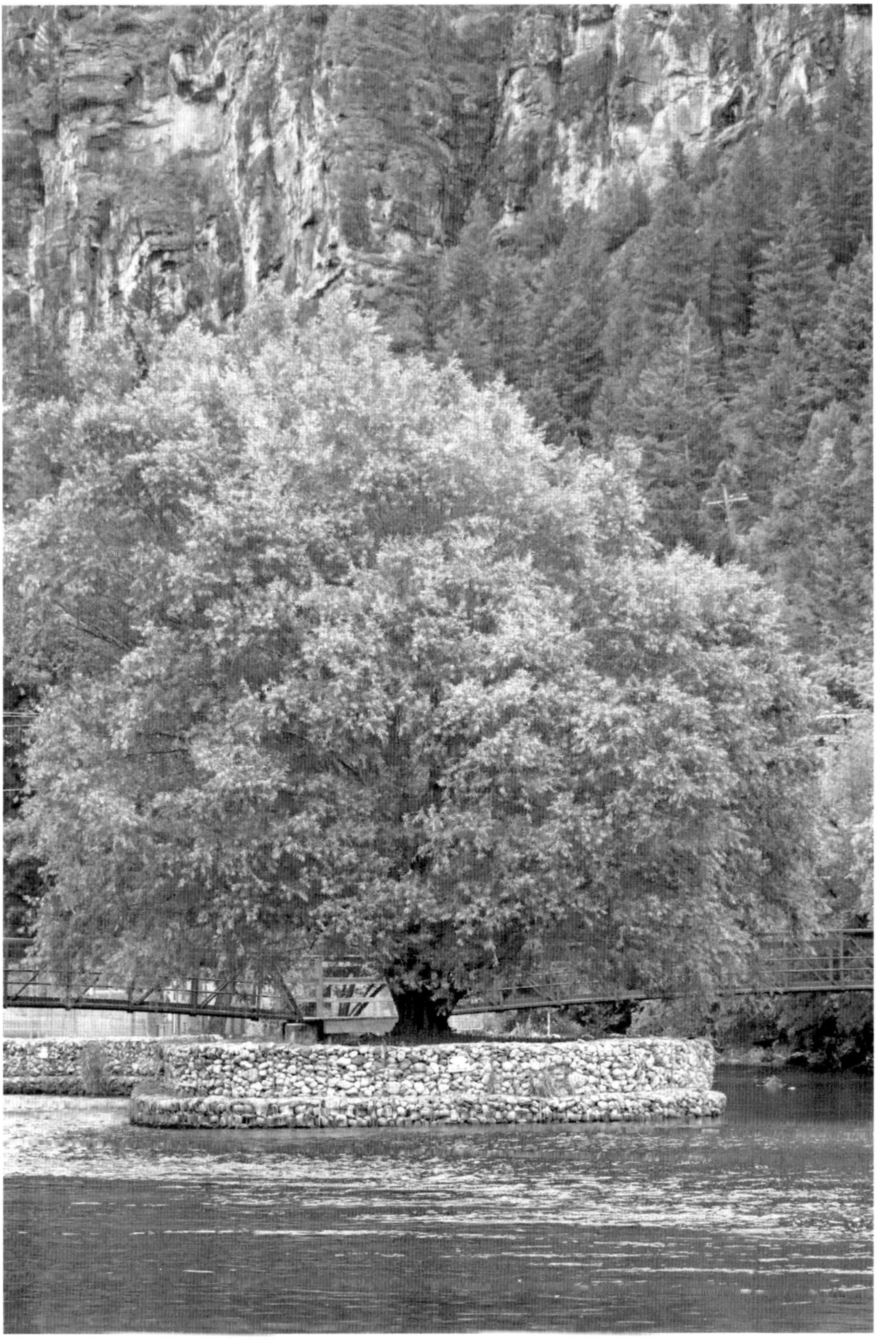

A scene from First Dam in Logan Canyon. *Author photo.*

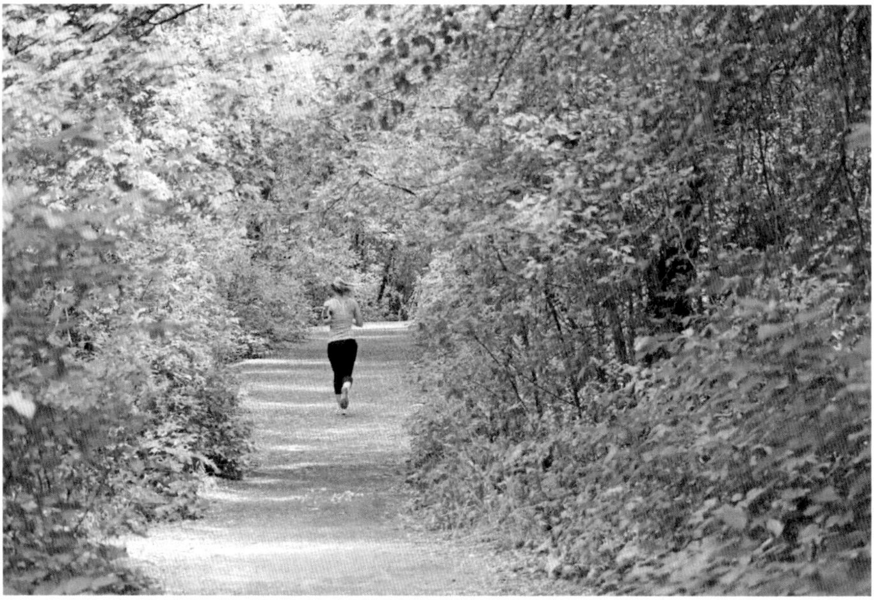

A runner on a river trail in Logan Canyon. *Author photo.*

Maguire primrose but not enough for the flower to grant it an easy life. Is there something a flower should learn from hard work?

At the base of the word *primrose* is the word *prim*, which came into use at the end of the seventeenth century. The Oxford English Dictionary says that to be prim is "to assume a formal, precise, or demure air." That's what the Maguire primrose reminds me of—a butler or statesman standing thin and straight like a rail. On spring days in April, when the flower is in full bloom, it looks down from its precarious limestone home. Below the cliff is a curious rushing. U.S. Highway 89 slaloms next to, over and across the Logan River at the canyon's base, and the Maguire primrose is witness. It witnesses the futility of our hustling here and there, our hauling, construction and recreation. It has been witness to our arrogant attempts to tame a mountain using our ten tiny fingers, and it simply spreads out its petals, smiling in response.

As happened in so many other areas, the local rangers quickly took exception to this new, seemingly aggressive user group, especially in its potential to negatively affect the Maguire primrose. Years ago, when I lived in Logan, I worked on a project by the Mountain West Center for Regional Studies. They wanted to create an oral history of land use in Logan Canyon. We were sent out with recording equipment and a list of phone numbers and addresses for people who had been influential in the canyon's history. One of the names on my list was Scott Bushman, a former Forest Service fire chief. At one point in my conversation with Bushman, we hit on the topic of sport climbing. "I was against it. I was not just against it; I was passionately against it," stated Bushman, a trad climber himself.[10] One of the issues Bushman felt they could use to help control the development of sport climbing in Logan Canyon was the presence of the Maguire primrose.

Through a series of sit-down meetings, the growing climbing community—including climbers like Cupal; his wife at the time, Deb Cupal; Sinclair; Sherner; Monsell; and Doug Heinrich, among others—was able to come to an understanding with the Forest Service and establish a climbing management plan that would restrict bolting or climbing to areas away from the presence of the Maguire primrose but still allow climbers to develop new routes elsewhere. For the climbers, this meant giving up some established climbs, like *Hobbit Hole* (5.8, FA unavailable), *Standard Direct* (5.10 a/b, FA unavailable) and Bob Sinclair's 5.12, which may have been the first true sport route in the canyon, as well as some undeveloped walls that may have held promising projects. All in all, it was a concession the climbers were willing to make. In a way, Logan climbers almost became protectors of the little flower. Every guidebook I've ever seen for Logan Canyon, including the most recent one by Casey Hyer, *Northern Utah Limestone Climbing*, contains a section about the Maguire primrose and how climbers should not only stay away from climbs that have been marked for the flower but also report to the Forest Service new locations where the Magwire primrose has spread. So we sacrifice, if you can call it that, a small portion of our recreational ease while we work for a productive relationship between nature, with its finicky needs, and man, with our desire for self-exploration.

According to Cupal, the management plan also contained a stipulation that no new routes be established within fifty feet of each other. As Cupal notes, "Honestly, that was just flat out ignored because if you find a good wall that's fifty feet wide, you're doing pretty good, and you'll want to put several routes on it."

After three or four years, Logan Canyon did catch the eye of climbers from Salt Lake City and down to the Provo area, people like the aforementioned Bill Boyle. This surge of out-of-town developers added depth to the canyon's route offerings. The China Wall Cave, which sits right next to the Bolt Ladder, became the home of several ambitious projects, including one by Boyle's fellow American Fork Canyon climber Boone Speed. Speed's route *Super Tweak* would become the first 5.14b in America.[11]

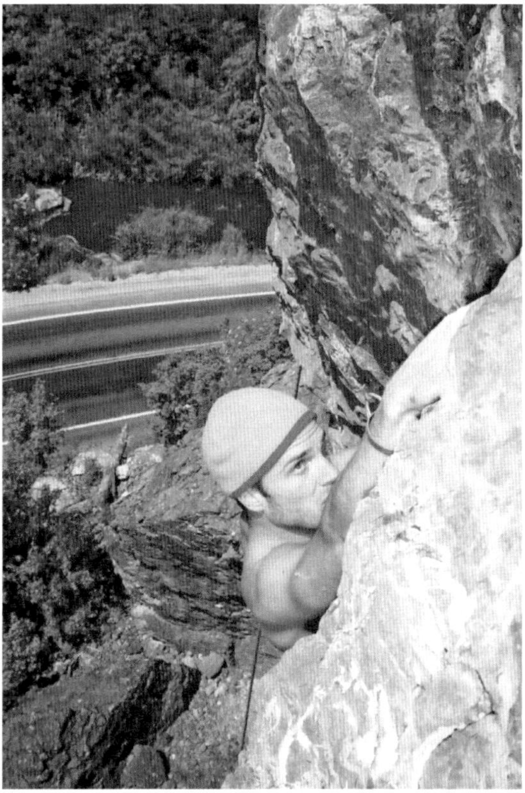

An image of me leading *Hat Trick* 5.11b, 385 area, Logan Canyon. *Photo by Emily Marsh.*

Even after the out-of-towners left, the effect of showing that stone as steep as that in the China Wall Cave could be climbed continued to influence the way local route developers, such as Doug Walker, Psyd Wright, Chuck Odette and Casey Hyer, looked at the canyon. They carried that mentality of pushing difficulty levels with them as they developed new areas, like Choss Cave, Solar Cave and the Tidal Wave Cave. (I was once bitten by a spider while climbing in the Tidal Wave Cave and ended up in the emergency room with EMTs laughing at my swollen uvula—fun times!)

Perhaps this gradual evolution of sport climbing in Logan Canyon is why there is such a balanced range of climbs. In some canyons, it can be difficult to take a group of climbers who are at different ability levels out together. A wall that has multiple options for the beginner will have nothing to challenge the more experienced climber. However, that was rarely a problem for me in Logan. It seemed wherever we went, there was something for everyone to do and something no one could do.

Another benefit of a slow but steady pace of route development in Logan Canyon is that it has helped the climbing community avoid having many of the environmental impact problems that some other areas have seen. Of course, a perk for local developers is that you don't have to worry about another climber stealing your project. As Cupal pointed out, "I moved away a little while and then moved back about three years ago, and some of the routes I saw way back when were still here waiting to be done. So that was kind of cool."

The MPRP says it is not "feasible" that the Maguire primrose will ever be removed from the endangered and threatened species list "given the species' very small natural population, limited habitat, and the persistent nature of potential threats." Yes, road construction will continue, amateur horticulture collecting and rock climbing will go on, and winter will continue to fall on Cache County. But despite all this, the Maguire primrose blooms. It refuses to listen to the odds and continues on the way it did before the settling of this valley, or the recreationalization of its canyon. The Maguire primrose couldn't care less for us and continues on the way it did for centuries before we ever knew about it, before our need to worry about everything drove us to coddle it. Of course, that's the catch: if it weren't for our need to worry about everything, our drive to explore and create would have finished the Maguire primrose off years ago. So we continue pushing our boundaries, fretting all the way.

6
OGDEN CANYON

If I were to write a chapter on climbing of any kind in the Ogden area and not mention the Lowes, two things would happen. One, I would be doing a huge disservice to the history of rock climbing in that area. Two, I very well might find a mob of angry climbers outside my door one day.

That said, this chapter isn't about the Lowes just like this book isn't about trad climbing.

The Tintic Quartzite in Ogden is, by nature, fractured. It wears splits and cracks like club boys and girls wear glitter, and, just like the glitter, the features tend to catch the eye. "It's so fractured here that you can almost always wiggle something in, even if it's just a little nest of microwires," said David G. Robb, author of the *Ogden Area Climbing Guide*. I'd guess this is part of why the Lowes found themselves rock climbing in the Ogden area so often. Everywhere you look, there is something to do, a new line to try up every cliff.

Over time, the abundance of features in which the creative climber could place gear led to a dilemma. It became difficult to know who had done what first. When in doubt, local climbers knew to give a nod to the Lowes. As Robb mentioned to me, someone could think they had discovered a brand-new trad route only to find, upon reaching the top of the cliff, that another climber had already set up an anchor or left a piton. Time, sweat and no doubt some amount of blood spent working their way up a series of cracks and fissures could all be done in vain regardless of how careful the ambitious first ascensionist was. This is, according to Robb, the reason he didn't include first assent information in his guidebook. The way I met Robb is a perfect

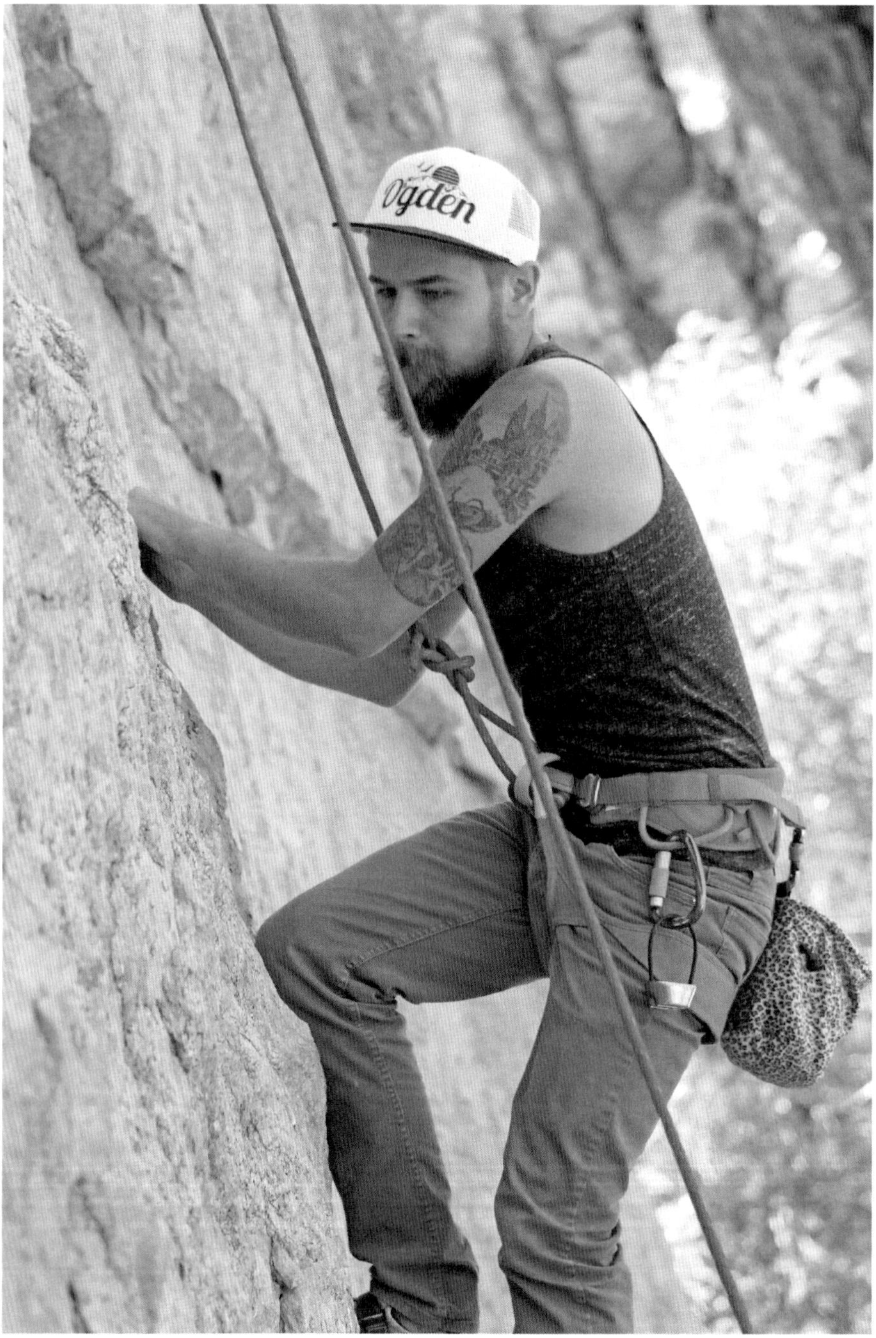

An unknown local climbing in Ogden Canyon. *Author photo.*

example of how I like to live—with my foot as close to my mouth as possible (unsurprisingly, my son, just a newborn, has this same habit).

One of the first things I did when researching an area, especially those I had climbed in but knew little to nothing about, was to dig into the area's guidebook. Not only do most guidebooks contain first ascent information, which can be crucial in figuring out where to start research, but they also often feature short histories in their introductions. While I like Robb's *Ogden Area Climbing Guide*, it wasn't doing much to help me out. On my state-long photo trip, I talked to a few dozen climbers in Ogden, none of whom could offer me anything beyond "the Lowes, man." My research had hit a very frustrating quartzite wall.

During this same time, I had the chance to teach a couple of workshops at the annual League of Utah Writers writing conference. Halfway through my second workshop, this one on the topic of writing poetry, a man a little bit older and a little bit taller than me walked in and sat at the back of the room. The workshop went like it had the other hundred times I'd taught it. Afterward, a few writers hung around to ask questions or to talk to me about their projects. When they'd all cleared out, the man who'd come in during the middle of the workshop approached me. "Hi, great workshop," he started. "I mean, I'm not a poet, but I enjoyed it." When I asked him why he'd attended the workshop if he wasn't particularly interested in writing poetry, he answered that he was a rock climber and had noticed that my bio in the workshop program said that I was writing a book about sport climbing. I told him that I was, and we talked about how the book was going. I asked him where he liked to climb. "Mostly in Ogden," he said.

"Oh, I've been having a tough time researching Ogden. The guidebook author didn't include any first ascent info," I said with just a touch of frustration. He tilted his head a little and looked at me with what I can best describe as sympathetic awkwardness as he said, "Oh, ah, I wrote that."

Have I mentioned yet that there is a lot of ego in climbing? Because there is *a lot* of ego in climbing. It wouldn't have surprised me at all if Robb had told me to go screw myself, but he didn't. He very graciously explained why he'd written the book the way he had and offered to be of any help he could. A few days later, I had a lengthy and enjoyable conversation with Robb over the phone. We talked about trad climbing in Ogden and how it had been so dominant due to the nature of the rock. Of course for all the trad routes people—Lowes or otherwise—had established, there were always those boring blank spaces between the cracks.

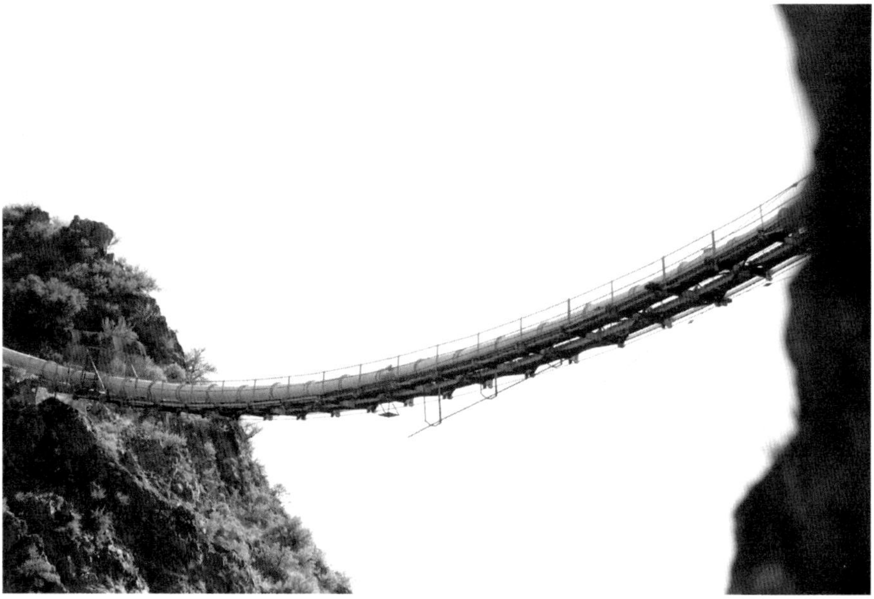

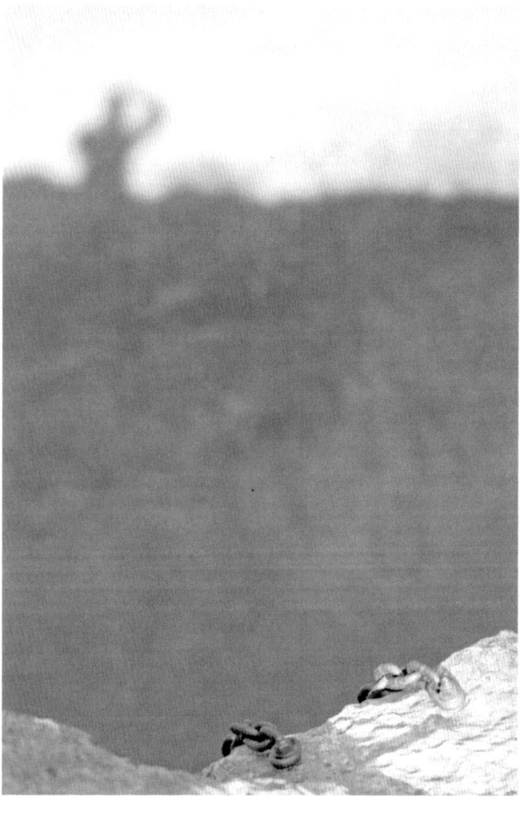

Above: A suspension water pipe crosses over Ogden Canyon. *Author photo.*

Left: My shadow as seen from the top of a roadside crag in Ogden Canyon. *Author photo.*

Cracks were exciting. They were steps in a treasure map. With no features to place gear in, the blank rock faces between them sat undisturbed. The mindset in climbing had been, it seems, largely focused on gear and gear placement. With that mindset spread among the broader climbing community, people saw what they wanted to and discounted anything else. In fact, in many areas, a period existed where bolts were solely used to bridge short sections of face climbing that lay between two sections of trad climbing. Eventually, the paradigm began to shift. Suddenly those boring blank sections of rock weren't only interesting; they had opened up an entirely new world of possibilities, even in areas where locals felt that everything had already been done.

It is easy to do this, as people, to walk through our days seeing only what we're looking for from out of the noise that makes up the world around us. And the world can be a noisy, busy mess. If we try to take too much of it in at once, we can lose focus on the really important things like paying rent or the mortgage, saving for that retirement when we think we'll do all the things we don't have time for now. Those are the really important things, right? Follow the path you've seen everyone else take. Don't stand out or go against the group.

As Mike Pleinis, the first climber to make the bold move of bolting a sport route in Ogden—and one hell of a climbing historian—explained, "The word sport climbing was originally a pejorative." He recalled at one point seeing a bumper sticker that said, "Sport Climbing Is Neither." In speaking about trad climbing and the older ethic, he went on to add, "It was a lifestyle. It was a spiritual thing. It wasn't sport, not to a lot of us."

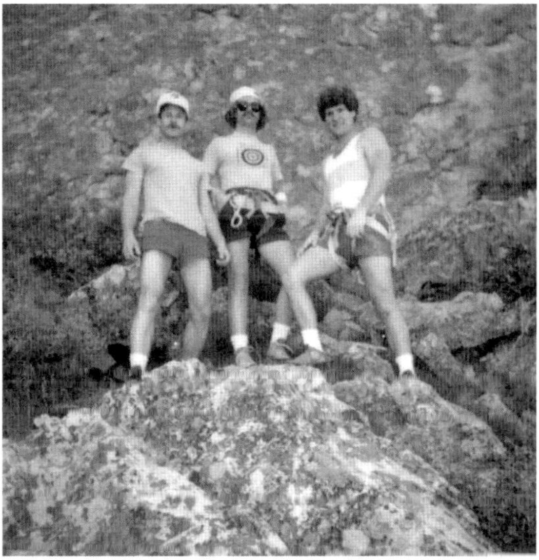

(Left to right) Mike Pleinis, Joe Cupps and Tim Bratten stand at the base of a climb in Ogden, 1990. *Courtesy of Mike Pleinis.*

Pleinis first gained an interest in climbing in college. As the climbing ethic began to change—or, let's say, evolve—from a trad-only mentality, his own paradigm shifted a little, making room for elements of sport climbing. Suddenly, he started to notice those spaces between the cracks. Pleinis, who read *Rock and Ice* and *Climbing* with as much zeal as the average Utahan might read the *Book of Mormon*, decided to try some of the techniques he'd read that the French and Italians were doing. Whatever debate there was around the ethics of the sport climbing trend that the French and Italian climbers had started, there could be little to no argument that since they'd started using bolting and sport climbing techniques, as Pleinis put it, "they were kicking our asses in technical ability."

There are several reasons that sport climbing and rap bolting allowed these foreign climbers to advance in ability. They enabled them to rehearse routes, doing them repeatedly on top rope before trying them on lead, and it allowed them to experiment safely on far more challenging climbs.

During this time, Pleinis, who'd moved from Texas to Utah in January 1985 to work for Western Zirconium, had gone from practicing bouldering in hiking boots in the fields above Saint Joe's to driving down to Salt Lake City to take climbing classes from epic Salt Lake City climber Merrill Bitter. Through his bouldering efforts, Pleinis had met local Bob Ellis, whom he started climbing with. Through Ellis he would eventually meet Hack (a nickname given, apparently, for his chain smoking) and Dave Black, who Pleinis described as being "considered king of the climbing community around [Ogden]."

Eventually, Pleinis would buy a Petzel hand drill. He was well aware of the bolt wars going on in the states and the ethical debates those were creating. For himself, he'd decided on a sort of modified ethic. Climbing and bolting sport routes were OK, as long as he tried to stick as close to the older ethic as possible: no placing bolts anywhere that he could fit even a small nut, no rap bolting unless necessary. As he told me, "I was steadfastly opposed to bolting cracks. I was steadfastly opposed to any kind of chipping or gluing [holds]." So in May 1987, Pleinis headed up to Utah Canyon, a small side canyon off Ogden Canyon, to a nice blank stone face that was close to the road, providing a convenient approach, and bolted, from what I could dig up, the first sport route in Ogden.

He started by using a crack on the left of the face to climb up to a small ledge that he could traverse to reach the route he wished to establish. From the ledge, trying to bolt ground up, Pleinis hammered at the rock and cranked on that Petzel hand drill until he was able, after about an hour, to put a quarter-inch button-head bolt in the wall. The process was exhausting. If he was going to establish the route the way it should be in his mind, he was going to have to switch to rap bolting, a step he took with some trepidation, unsure how longtime locals like Dave

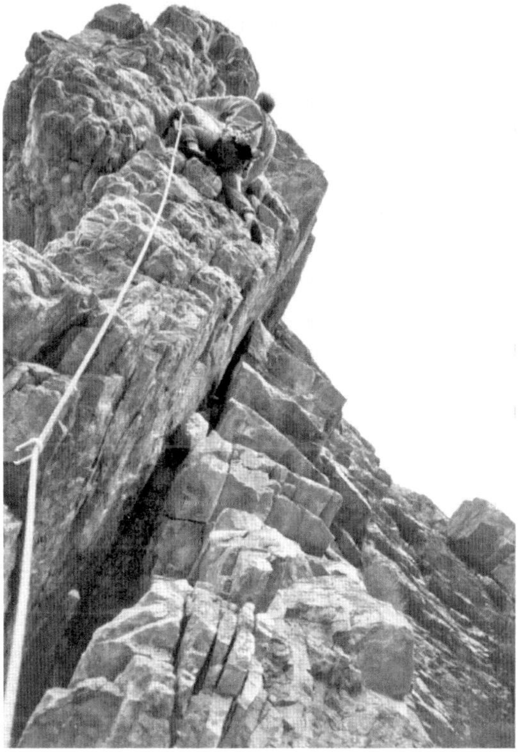

Mike Pleinis leads *Air Time*, Ogden Canyon, 1991. *Courtesy of Mike Pleinis.*

Black would react to such a move. His car parked right by the climb, Pleinis listened to the radio as he worked. At one point, the old Warren Zevon song "Lawyers, Guns, and Money" came on, and when he heard the line "I'm hiding in Honduras, the shit has hit the fan, send lawyers, guns, and money," he thought it a fitting name for the climb since he might need to hit the road and hide, depending on how the community reacted to his effort.

Once he told them what he'd done, he was pleasantly surprised that no one much seemed to care. No one raced up there to chop his bolts as he'd read of happening in so many other places. With the confidence this gave him, Pleinis would continue climbing with his new mixed ethic. Soon, other climbers began bolting, too. Ray West established a route at the Perry Camp area on a slab called Delusion Flake, but he placed a bolt too close to where Black thought a piece of trad gear could be used, and that bolt did get chopped.

Pleinis wasn't as epic in his breadth of creation as many of the bolting pioneers in other areas were. He didn't put up hundreds upon hundreds of routes like Pedersen, Boyle and Speed. He didn't get first ascents all across the globe like James Garret. He would put up a handful of mixed-gear routes in the area he named Upper Utah Wall, among a few others. What he should be noted for is, perhaps, opening the eyes and broadening the ethic of an entire community of climbers or at least starting them down that path.

Years later, Pleinis would return to find that someone had retro bolted one of his mixed-aid routes. The bolt they had added was in a section Pleinis

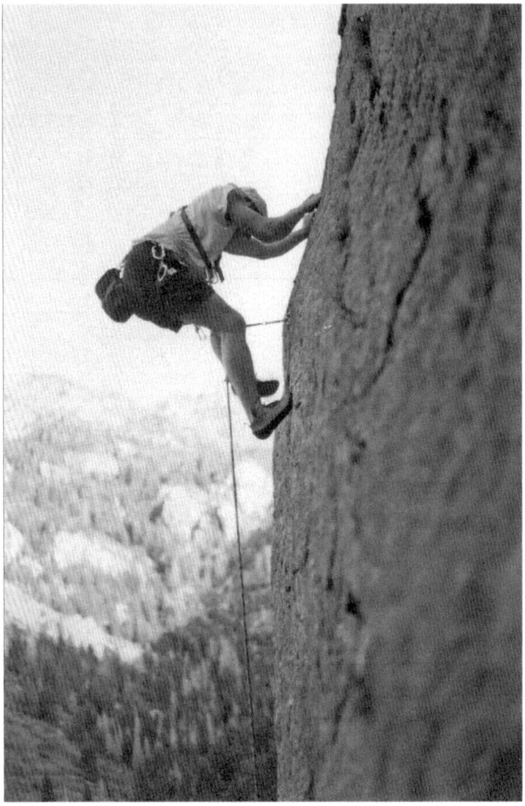

Mike Pleinis leads *Delusion Flake Arete*, Ogden Canyon, late 1980s. *Photo by Nate Rydman.*

had specifically left blank since there was a spot in the rock for a nut. So, he got up on the climb and chopped the new bolt. He was sure to back-fill the hole to leave as little impact on the rock as possible, a practice not carried out by all climbers who took it upon themselves to chop bolted routes. Afterward, Pleinis would go down to the Black Diamond shop in the middle of Ogden and relate the story to his friends who worked there. In turn, one of them created a wanted sign asking for any information on who the retro bolter might be. Whoever it was, he or she was never found.

While Pleinis's reaction was based partly in trying to maintain the core of a more traditional climbing ethic, one might argue that it was also based, in part, as a reaction to an artist seeing someone edit their work.

I've always seen sport routes as works of art and their developers as artists, whether they intended to be or not. The process of establishing a sport route, of bolting a line up a cliff face, is part art and part athleticism. Like a sculptor, the route setter must pick away at the stone. They must see past what is there to what it can be, but these sculptures are interactive. The setter's creation only comes to life when someone engages with it. While I can see the line of bolts that mark the path a climber must take to finish *Lawyers, Guns, and Money*, could it be that the true art is in how each climber interacts with Pleinis's creation? Watching people crane their bodies to the right, both hands clinging to a side pull, their left foot hiked up by their waist as they pull themselves up past a bulge of stone—is this the work of art coming to life?

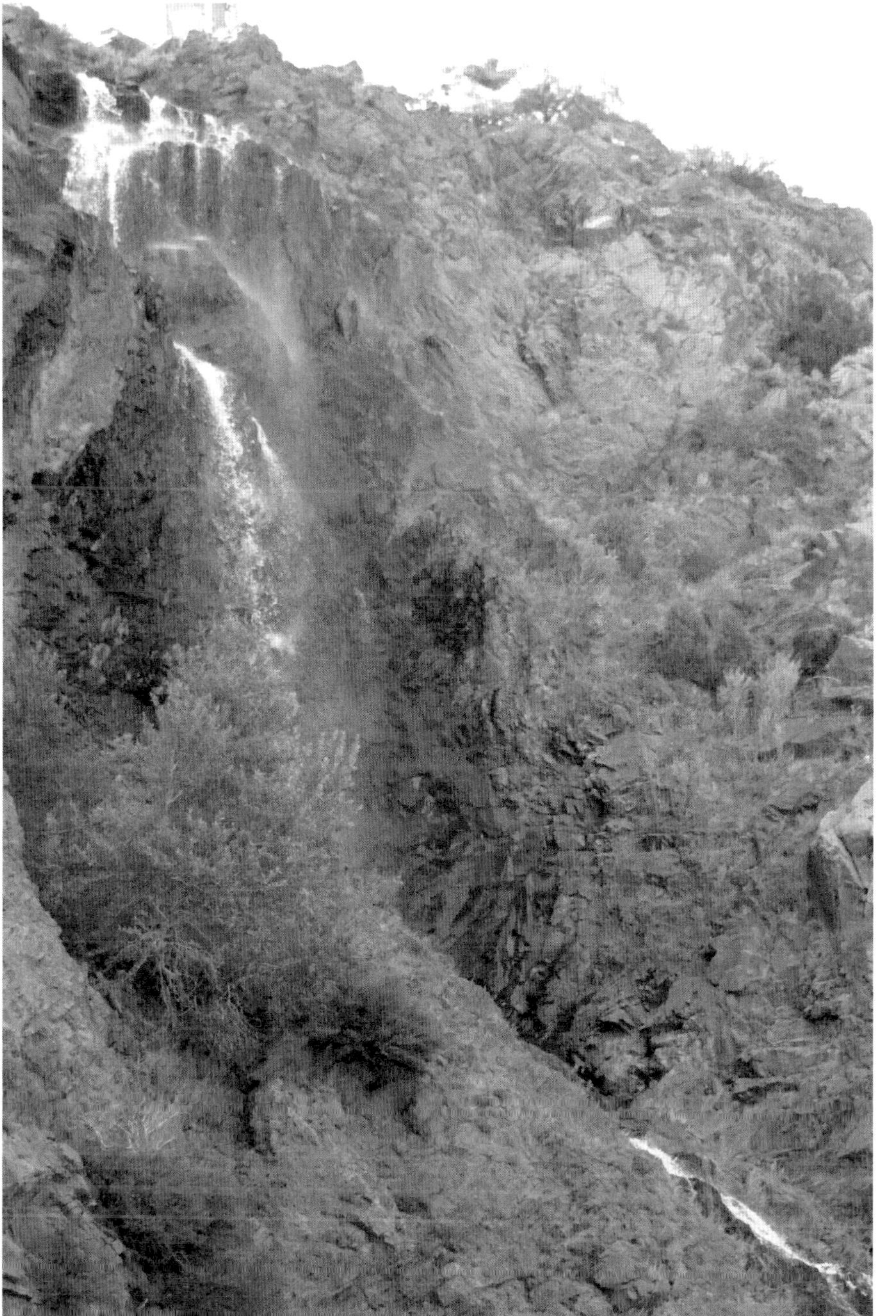

Water cascades down Ogden Canyon Falls. *Author photo.*

Others might say it is the path chosen up the rock itself, the imaginary line strung between two-inch metal bolts, not the way each climber moves up them, that holds the art. Could it be both? Or, does the true work of art exist only as long as the process of creation?

San Francisco Beat artist Jay Defeo believed the only important part of art is its creation, the finished product being just an echo of the artistic experience. In this light, each time climbers approach a route, we could say they prepare to create their own work of art, a work that will burn off into time as soon as they've rappelled back down. However, nearly every developer I spoke with shied away from being compared to an artist, as if the term "artist" were too lofty a title.

Artists interact with the world, through whatever medium, in a way that adds beauty and complexity to it, in a way that can enrich the lives of others who interact with it. There is a reason climbing magazines and blogs are full of pictures of people climbing. There is something beautiful about the way the human body interacts with the stone. And certainly, the lives of the climbers who are able to challenge themselves, push their own limits on someone else's creation, are enriched by the process. Can't we then say that the dedicated and thoughtful route developer is, indeed, an artist?

Shortly after the initial bolting efforts, Ogden Canyon went into a downtime. People forgot about their hometown crags for the more exciting things happening up in Logan Canyon. And it was understandable. This would have been around the same time that Boone Speed was establishing *Super Tweak* at the China Wall Cave in Logan Canyon. *Super Tweak* was the first 5.14d in America, a major breakthrough in American sport climbing, and yet another draw to put Utah sport climbing on the national and international stages. I imagine everyone in Ogden would have wanted to be part of that excitement. They would have wanted to be a part of that history, to go check out the insanely overhanging work that climbers like Speed were doing in Logan. So they stopped exploring their hometown crags and took the short drive forty-five minutes north, through Sardine Canyon and the cow pastures of Logan, Utah; past Utah State University; and into the limestone heaven of Logan Canyon.

It would be years before sport climbing in the Ogden area would catch a second wind.

That wind would come at the hands of Michael Anderson. Anderson revolutionized sport climbing in the Ogden area and rejuvenated the local sport climbing community. Anderson, like myself, started climbing in the Boy Scouts and then continued on his own. At the time, he lived in Oregon. Life

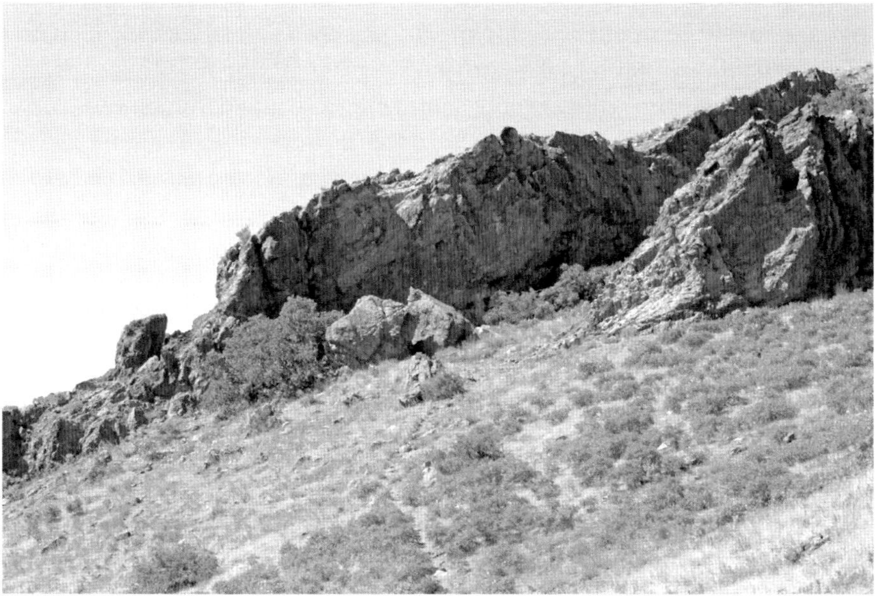

The Ninth Street Crag in Ogden is one of the most popular sport climbing locations for locals. *Author photo.*

took him to Colorado, where he bolted his first sport route, before it brought him to Ogden, Utah. That move came in 1999, when he moved to Ogden for his work in the air force. Upon arriving in Ogden, Anderson found that the only climbing scene was at the local gym, and it wasn't very big. Later, he met local Ogden climber Mark Springer while climbing Nailen's Falls (an ice climb), and Springer put him in touch with more climbers.

Anderson lived in Utah for five years and developed routes in the Ogden area for three of those. He developed the School Room Wall with Brent Hadley and many other areas. His efforts showed locals that there was still a lot to be proud of as far as climbing goes in the Ogden area. There was still a lot to do.

After leaving Utah, Anderson moved to Colorado Springs, where he was once again a newcomer. Dedicated to climbing and pushing his own limits, he developed an intensive training routine. In 2006, he started publishing some of the exercises and techniques online. By 2011, he'd started putting them together for a book. Then, in April 2014, his training book for climbing, *The Rock Climber's Trainin Manual*, was published and received an outstanding reception.

Anderson looked at sport climbing the way few others had, as something like basketball or football that could have an entire training program dedicated to it. I'm sure this idea might turn the stomachs of some of the old-school "Sport Climbing Is Neither" group, but it has aided many people in pushing themselves in much the same way his route development has. If we always accept things as they are, we never move into new territory. Pleinis would have never bolted *Lawyers, Guns, and Money*. Anderson would have never looked for more sport routes in the Ogden area than already existed when he moved there in 1999. All the people who have been able to use Anderson's training program to push both their climbing and themselves further might have been stuck hang dogging where they were. But thanks to people like Pleinis and Anderson and all the other route developers who weren't happy just taking what they were given, everything has moved forward a step, and the world is better for it.

7
WASATCH RANGE

As an area, the Salt Lake Valley has transformed from a Mormon pioneer settlement to a cosmopolitan city faster and more smoothly than the rest of Utah. Despite the popular perception of Salt Lake City as nothing more than the Mormon capital of the world—oftentimes a place rife with sister wives and a bit of an Amish vibe in the minds of out-of-staters—it has one of the country's strongest LGBT communities. *PRIDE* magazine named it the Gayest City in America in 2013.

People here have learned that paradigm shifts aren't bad; rather, they are essential. The early Catholic, Protestant, atheist and Jewish individuals who made Salt Lake City their home were faced with a sharp cultural shock upon moving to the valley. Regardless of what they were before moving here, there were all now the "other," a group lumped together under a label that identified them by what they weren't, Mormon, instead of what they were. Some of these non-Mormons converted to the Latter-day Saint (Mormon) faith, but all of them had to learn to adapt in some way. They were forced to see the world differently, to reevaluate their constants. While this transition might be easier today, it is still very much present for anyone who tries to transplant themselves into the state. At my day job as the managing editor of the *Southern Utah Independent*, I hear stories about this struggle all of the time. I'm not picking on Mormons, either. Anytime the majority of an area's population is made up of individuals with the same mindset, views and beliefs, there is going to be a divide between them and the minority. How strong that divide is and how elegantly it is bridged, I imagine, would depend greatly on the people within a given community.

Back when I worked in education, as part of teaching my English 1010 students about denotation and connotation, I often used "reevaluate" and "questioning" as examples of words whose connotation, perhaps unfairly, clashes with their denotation. These words have picked up a distinctly negative connotation. When someone says that they are questioning their marriage or faith, the instinctual response is to gasp, "Oh, no!"

But why?

Questions needn't be scary things. If I tell someone that I've been questioning my marriage or if you say that you're reevaluating your religion, it doesn't mean that either of those institutions are in peril. I could be asking, "Why is my wife so wonderful?" You might be reevaluating where your faith sits in your life and how you can make it more of an integral part day by day.

Indeed, for the non-Mormon settlers of the Salt Lake Valley, this process of questioning, reevaluating the way they saw the world, often left them rooted more firmly where they already stood, though, perhaps it enabled them to see different colors scattered across the landscape as well. The Mormon settlers who found themselves suddenly infiltrated by nonbelievers likewise needed to struggle through the process of seeing things differently. If they were going to maintain relative peace as a community, the Mormons couldn't look at all outsiders as a threat.

Tolerance and acceptance are two distinct routes to this goal. One, tolerance, requires no understanding on the part of the majority. The landscape of their reality might change but only as much as redirecting a trail around a rattlesnake's den. Acceptance (which it's important to note is not the same thing as agreement) requires the dominant group to come to some understanding of the new group(s), to no longer see them as poisonous snakes but as fellow human beings.

Perhaps the people in Salt Lake City adapted faster than the rest of the state because they didn't have as much time to insulate themselves from outside forces. Places like Provo and Manti didn't receive the same influx of "gentiles," and as such, they were given more time to cement their view of the world. As Jennifer Michael Hect says in her book *Doubt: A History*, "Difference alone leads to a more questioning, critical attitude toward received truths, i.e., truths that have tradition as their primary proof or source of authority."[12] This is what Hect calls a cosmopolitan doubt.

The ethical transition of the Salt Lake City climbing community from a trad climbing–only philosophy to accepting, first, a ground-up bolting philosophy and then, later, the practice of bolting on rappel could serve as a petri dish for exploring these rather large ideas in a much more manageable setting.

For Salt Lake City climbers like Merrill Bitter, Hank Armantrout, Drew Bedford and the Ruckman brothers—Bret and Stuart—bolting seemed, from what I've been able to dig up, to evolve as a natural outgrowth of trad climbing. Like many areas, Salt Lake City held on to aspects of the older climbing ethic, many of them I believe rightly so. For example, it is seen as crossing an ethical line to add bolts to a route someone else has established or to bolt over an existing trad route. Sadly, there are examples of both of these forms of retro-bolting happening in many Salt Lake City climbing areas. One such instance happened in Ferguson Canyon, a side canyon at the mouth of Big Cottonwood Canyon.

Ferguson Canyon has a fair bit of lore itself. The story goes that during the earliest days of Mormon settlers in the Salt Lake Valley, a group of pioneers came to their prophet, Brigham Young, about a gold vein they'd discovered up what is now Ferguson Canyon. Fearing the migration of non-Mormons, which would soon come anyway, Young told the men to bury their find and to never mention it to anyone. It seems this type of folklore always ends that way, with an order of silence that obviously goes unheeded. So now, bored high school students go up Ferguson Canyon looking for the lost Ferguson gold mine.

If they're paying attention, what they'll find is an abundance of climbing. Ferguson was one of the earliest areas in Salt Lake City to be bolted. As early as 1983, the same year Allen Watts bolted *Watts Tots* at Smith Rock in Oregon, Drew Bedford and Hank Armantrout were bolting routes like *Dark Rose* (5.11c, FA Drew Bedford and Hank Armantrout),[13] *Total Ramon* (5.11c, FA Drew Bedford and Hank Armantrout) and *Draw the Line* (5.9, FA Hank Armantrout, Bill Cramer and Dave Casey). Like elsewhere, many of the routes in Ferguson are mixed aid, meaning here that they were intended as a trad route but had a section of stone where no gear could be placed.

One of the trad climbs that, as the Ruckmans put it, "now has four bolts, placed by a clueless climber,"[14] is *Nuptial Vow* (5.8, FA Les Ellison, Paul Scannel and Brian Smoot).

This is a spot where I find myself torn. I agree 100 percent with the ethic that the "clueless" climber was in the wrong. That line was done by Ellison, Scannel and Smoot. The art was created by them. Still, however wrong the climber was (and he or she was wrong), it has opened that work of art to a broader audience. While spending an afternoon talking to climbers and getting photos up Ferguson Canyon, I spotted two groups of young climbers on the north face of the Cathedral. While one group had trad gear on their slings, the second had only quick draws. I watched them climb *Nuptial Vow*, and they seemed to truly enjoy it. Had that route not been bolted, there is a chance that second group might not have been able to experience it. Of course, I could be wrong about those climbers. They could have had a stash of nuts and cams in one of their bags, but the idea still holds true.

I'd imagine there are hundreds of climbers (and, due to its easy rating, non-climbers) who have been able to interact with *Nuptial Vow* who wouldn't have been able to had the route never been bolted. So I can see where the argument that trad climbers should just do routes like *Nuptial Vow* while ignoring the bolts comes from, but I can't agree with it. Routes, trad or sport, are art to me. It takes an artist's eye to spot lines hidden in stone. With this in mind, bolting over someone's trad route is like a clueless local adding an extra swirl to the Spiral Jetty at the Great Salt Lake. These ethical issues the climbing community has had and continues to face aren't as simple as either side might make them appear.

It seems that the ethical transition in the Wasatch Range was eased by people just wanting to climb. Trad climbers took what they saw from the French and Italians and used it to link sections of protectable rock. So when they saw something they wanted to climb that wasn't protectable, they bolted the whole thing—simple logic. Just like the early settlers (Mormon and everyone else), it would seem that climbers in Salt Lake City learned early on that getting along and adapting is much easier and more productive than fighting.

8
MOAB

Moab, Utah, is a small town surrounded by big, big beauty. Situated close to both Arches National Park and Canyonlands National Park, Moab is the hub for everything outdoors in eastern Utah. It also has a distinct feel to it that you can't get anywhere else in the state. I'd say it's similar to Springdale, Utah, which sits at the mouth to Zion National Park, but where Springdale has a bit of soft glow, let's call it, to it, Moab seems to have some edge.

Trad climbing, aid climbing, big-wall climbing—the stories about those kind of adventures in Moab could fill several books, and have. Sport climbing, on the other hand, is a shorter story that's a lot harder to discover.

Noah Bigwood's parents taught him how to climb. This isn't that unusual a thing to hear now, in 2016. Hell, I've spent days in the climbing gym where it feels like a daycare. In fact, I hope to teach my own son to climb once he can walk. But pre-1990, this would have seemed like a strange idea to most people.

By high school, climbing had consumed Bigwood. He loved all the forms of climbing, from bouldering to sport and trad climbing. After attending college in Colorado, Bigwood, who had always felt drawn to the desert, moved to Moab, Utah. At this time, around 1994, the Millcreek area of Moab had seen the development of only eight to ten sport routes. While Millcreek wasn't necessarily the first sport climbing in Moab, it was, as Bigwood put it, "the first good-rock sport climbing." Before Millcreek, there had already been some bolting on Potash Road, a vertical stretch of cliff face

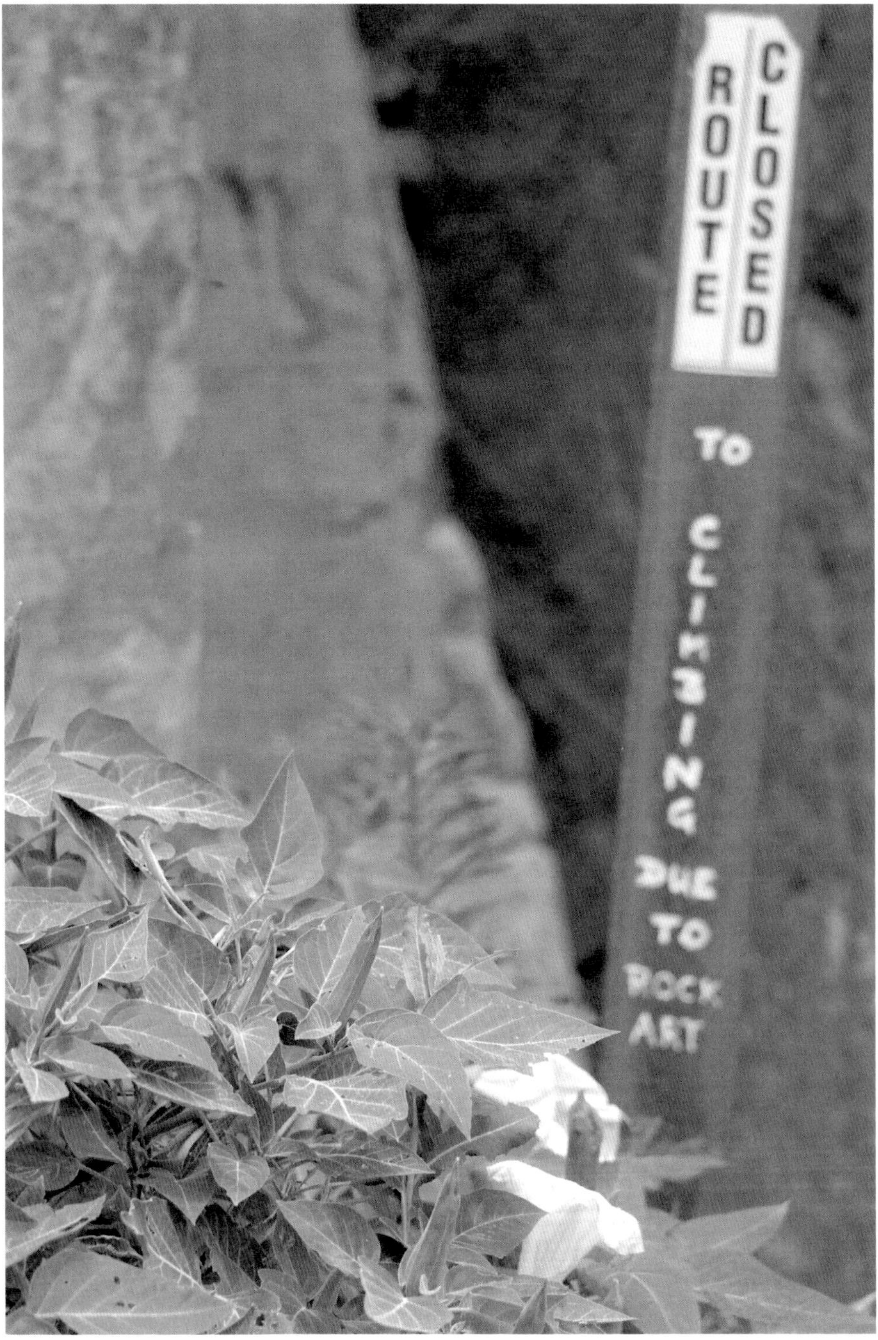

A "No Climbing" sign sits at the Wall Street Crag on Potash Road, Moab, Utah. *Author photo.*

north of Moab that has what you might call a park-and-climb approach. But, as Bigwood explains, "calling [Potash Road] sport climbing is a little bit of a misnomer. It was some funky stuff.…Everything has a spicy feel for being such a roadside crag, and the quality of the rock is pretty poor."

When people think of Moab and rock climbing, they don't picture bolts in a cliff face. For many people, the idea seems almost sacrilegious. In 2015, I took a research/photo trip to Moab with the goal of tracking down the names of the early sport climbers in the area and grabbing some shots of locals climbing. Unlike any other area I had researched, people seemed to clam up as soon as I mentioned sport climbing. In one gear shop that I visited, the climber behind the counter looked like he'd seen a ghost when I even said the words. In fact, after being repeatedly directed to Potash Road, where I met and got some photos of a lovely couple who were on a climbing trip through the States for their honeymoon, I finally skipped the gear shops and went to the Moab Visitor's Center, where a park ranger directed me to Millcreek.

Moab is big walls. It's high adventure, placing gear in a crack on a towering desert spire. It is not, at least on the surface, sport climbing.

This seems to be, at least in part, because locals want to protect and preserve the areas where sport climbing can be found. And, let's face it, sport climbers don't have the best reputation for preserving the areas they visit. I'm not saying the sport climbing community as a whole, or even as a majority, is that way, but you know what they say—a few bad apples can make the whole crate smell like shit. That is what they say, right?

And by all accounts, Millcreek is something worth being protective of, though I would hope everyone feels that way about their hometown crag. Remembering the first time he saw Millcreek, Bigwood noted, "When I was first introduced to Millcreek, it was a mind-blowing experience to see that quality of stone, that much untapped stone in such a pristine, beautiful canyon." As I dug around online, I found this to be a common reaction to the area. The word "magical" is used with some frequency.

While the desire of locals to protect a pristine area, to not let visitors who may not have respect for or an understanding of the area ruin it, is understandable, even admirable, things are rarely that simple.

Even more so than Snow Canyon in southern Utah, Moab climbers found themselves wrapped up in the conflict of the ethical debates between sport climbing and trad climbing, which soon evolved into ground-up bolting versus rap bolting. Speaking about the community's reaction to the development that began happening at Millcreek, Bigwood said, "It was very mixed, as you can imagine. There were a lot of what we call disgruntled trads who shunned Millcreek, shunned bolting. Then there was a lot of, I like to call it, confusion over bolting ethics."

The debate between ground-up bolting and rap bolting can often smell of an attempt by some to cling to, or even impose, a mindset that evolved in trad climbing. Conflict was frequent between climbers throughout the country in what is often called the Bolt Wars. But neither side's motives are ever as clear as they might make them seem, and change is almost always met with resistance.

Moab went through its own Bolt Wars. In expanding on the confusion he saw surrounding bolting ethics in Moab, Bigwood said, "The initial ethic in Millcreek was that everything was done from the ground up; however, it was ground up in a very backward way." He went on to explain how you approach the canyon from the rim, and climbers would put in anchors and rappel down, cleaning the route and picking holds. They might even go as far as doing the route on top rope first and then going back after all that and bolt it from the ground up. Bigwood admitted that he did his fair share of this but said he always pointed out that what they were doing wasn't ground-up bolting. He felt that some of this confusion was due to the fact that for many locals, this was their first experience bolting. "As a consequence, a lot of pretty bad bolting got done. There were some runouts that shouldn't have been put in," Bigwood recalled, later adding, "A lot of the time, the first, second and third bolt will all be ground falls. I would call that bad bolting." Still, there were some experienced route developers, like Tom Gilje, who tried to set the example for others, tried to set the mindset of young climbers like Eric Decaria and Tait Rees. Bigwood notes that one of the differences was that Gilje knew the line of good bolting and safety. He was able to walk right up to but not over it. Something it would take time for others to learn.

Eventually, things hit a boiling point. "There was definitely a lot of classic sport climbing crag bullshit," Bigwood summed up. Some routes were chopped, destroying and invalidating someone's work to force it to fit within their own paradigm of what climbing should be. "In the end, when it came down to real Bolt Wars, Dean [Potter] was [in] a camp of three or four people, then everyone else wanted things to be kind of live and let live." Potter, who died tragically in a wingsuit accident at Yosemite National Park in May 2015, was a storied free climber and alpinist who also took on challenges like base jumping. As Bigwood tells the story, things were reasonably peaceful between everyone at Millcreek until problems started between Potter and himself. "There were a few other players who were behind the scenes. Kevin Chase, who was the gear shop owner down there was sort of a rabble-rouser. He liked to kind of set people against one another." He went on, "Dean decided that I was not going to be his favorite guy. Long before I did any rappel bolting in there, he was getting up in my face." The first route that Bigwood put in on rappel, he says he did because doing it from the ground up wouldn't have given him the result that he wanted. I've found this to be common reasoning among route developers. You can select much better bolt placement on rappel. As a sport climber for over a decade, I know firsthand the difference bolt placement can make. There are routes where you find yourself awkwardly scrunched on a terrible hold as you try to reach and clip into a bolt that has been placed at an even worse angle from where you are. In sport climbing, you are never more vulnerable than you are when you're clipping. You are the farthest from your last bolt, your last point of protection; you have to take out extra slack for a moment in order to get the rope up to the clip; and you're doing this with only one hand on the wall.

Bigwood said he didn't try to keep the project a secret. He wasn't going to try to sneak it in there. So he bolted and climbed it. Others climbed it, too, and thought it was a great climb. Then, one day, it was gone. According to Bigwood, Potter had gone up and chopped it. At that, Bigwood said, "OK, that was my experiment. It got chopped. I won't be the one to go and put it back up but maybe somebody else will." Several months later, his friends Eric Decaria and Tom Gilje went up and rebolted the route on rappel. A few weeks after that, Gilje went back to Millcreek and happened to catch Potter in the act of rechopping the bolts. According to the story, there was a humorous moment where Gilje, an intimidating figure, stood at the top of the cliff yelling at Potter and then ran to the bottom of the cliff, yelling at Potter, and Potter, moving hand over hand, scrambled to the top of the climb and took off. I'm told that he would return later and chop several more routes that he mistakenly thought had been put up by Bigwood, one of which, according to Bigwood, Potter claimed shouldn't have bolts because he had free soloed it. Another route he claimed Bigwood had done on rappel but, according to Bigwood, had actually been done by local climber Lisa Hathaway from the ground up.

A few days later, hoping to put matters to rest, the climbing community held a sort of town hall where things nearly came to blows again between Potter and Gilje. While there is no evidence his decision was caused by the Bolt Wars, Potter would soon leave Moab to live in Yosemite (Yosemite would have a strong pull for a climber like Potter), though, he did return for several lengthy visits.

Eventually, things simmered down, but as Bigwood noted, there is still a lot of angst in the area. In his guidebook *High on Moab* (which is one of the most well-done guidebooks I've ever seen), Karl Kelley writes in regards to the bolting wars at Wall Street, a section of Potash Road: "Wall Street bolting wars. Enough already! You may feel you are doing the right thing but when it comes down to it you are just scarring the rock!"

So there is concern for the desert and forest that climbers love, a need to protect it from the uninitiated, to keep their pearl away from swine, but there also seems to be a desire to hold on to the mystique that surrounds Moab, the mystique built around the dazzling exposures and breathtaking adventure of trad climbing or free-soloing desert towers. There is also the sense of ownership people come to feel over an area they love that, though it was there long before they found it, anyone who comes after them must experience it the same way that they have. This is an idea that extends far beyond climbing.

I'm not trying to absolve the out-of-town sport climbers of wrongdoing. While I've rarely encountered it myself, and always to my dismay when I have, there are those sport climbers who'd rather treat our natural wonders like their local climbing gym, driving where they shouldn't to shorten the approach, leaving trash behind them when they're done (including human waste) and even dragging CD players out into the desert or woods and playing them at top volume regardless of the negative effect it might have on others trying to enjoy the area.

I've heard plenty of theories speculating why this happens. The most common is, at least for me, also the most frustrating. One of the things that makes sport climbing great is that it is a far more approachable way to climb. It makes the experiences you can only find picking your way up a cliff face or mountainside available to people who otherwise might not find them. However, because the doorway to sport climbing is so much wider than that of trad climbing, most people don't go through the unofficial initiation, of sorts, where you learn the social and ethical landscape associated with climbing. As a local Salt Lake City climber once said to me, "Someone who learns to climb in a gym goes outside expecting it to be like the gym and expecting that they can behave the same way they can at the gym." I would like to shrug this reputation off with the mindset that the idiots don't represent the whole, but that would be ducking the situation and would make us, the responsible sport climbers, part of the problem.

The last I checked, Millcreek doesn't appear in any guidebook, and I imagine any attempt to create a guide for the area would be met with some hostility. Still, the effort of locals to keep their gem hidden can go only so far in an age when anyone who wants to can put directions and route beta on the Internet. Locals, however pure or muddied their motives might be, can only plead and warn outsiders to respect the area should they come. Moab isn't the only area where this happens. It's common for the first people to discover a crag to want to keep it from the world, from the people behind the negative stereotypes.

Gym climbers, sport climbers, boulderers: it is up to us to pass on lessons of respect for the land and the other people who use it. It is up to us to correct the problems when we see them. Otherwise, we deserve the negative stereotypes that we feel have been unjustly placed on us. And our right to petition locals to share the areas they have claimed as their own becomes much harder to defend.

9
MAPLE CANYON

Maple Canyon, located just outside the small town of Fountain Green, Utah, and in proximity to Snow College in Ephraim, Utah, is one of the most mesmerizing places I've ever been. The cobblestones build in piles as high as mountains—well, they are mountains made up entirely of stones stuck together by sediment.

That's not the only reason that Maple Canyon is so remarkable. It's the way the side canyons have been formed, worn away by a winding river. Standing in the middle of Box Canyon—one of Maple's many side canyons—it's like standing in undertow watching waves rise above you. You're in the center of that storm of churning water, but everything has frozen.

The story I've usually heard about the early sport climbing development of Maple Canyon involves the likes of Jeff Pedersen, Bill Boyle, Darren Knezek and Bill Ohran, among other Utah County staples. If you tell their origin stories from the right angle, you could make most of the climbing areas in the state sound like they were spearheaded by that Utah County group. The truth is that after they'd established American Fork Canyon, those guys had their hands in a little bit of everything.

In January 1993, Pedersen and Ohran would open a small rock-climbing gear shop in Provo, Utah, called Mountainworks. It was located around the corner from a climbing gym started by some business students from Brigham Young University. That gym, called The Rock Garden, was where I had my first experience with climbing as a young Boy Scout.

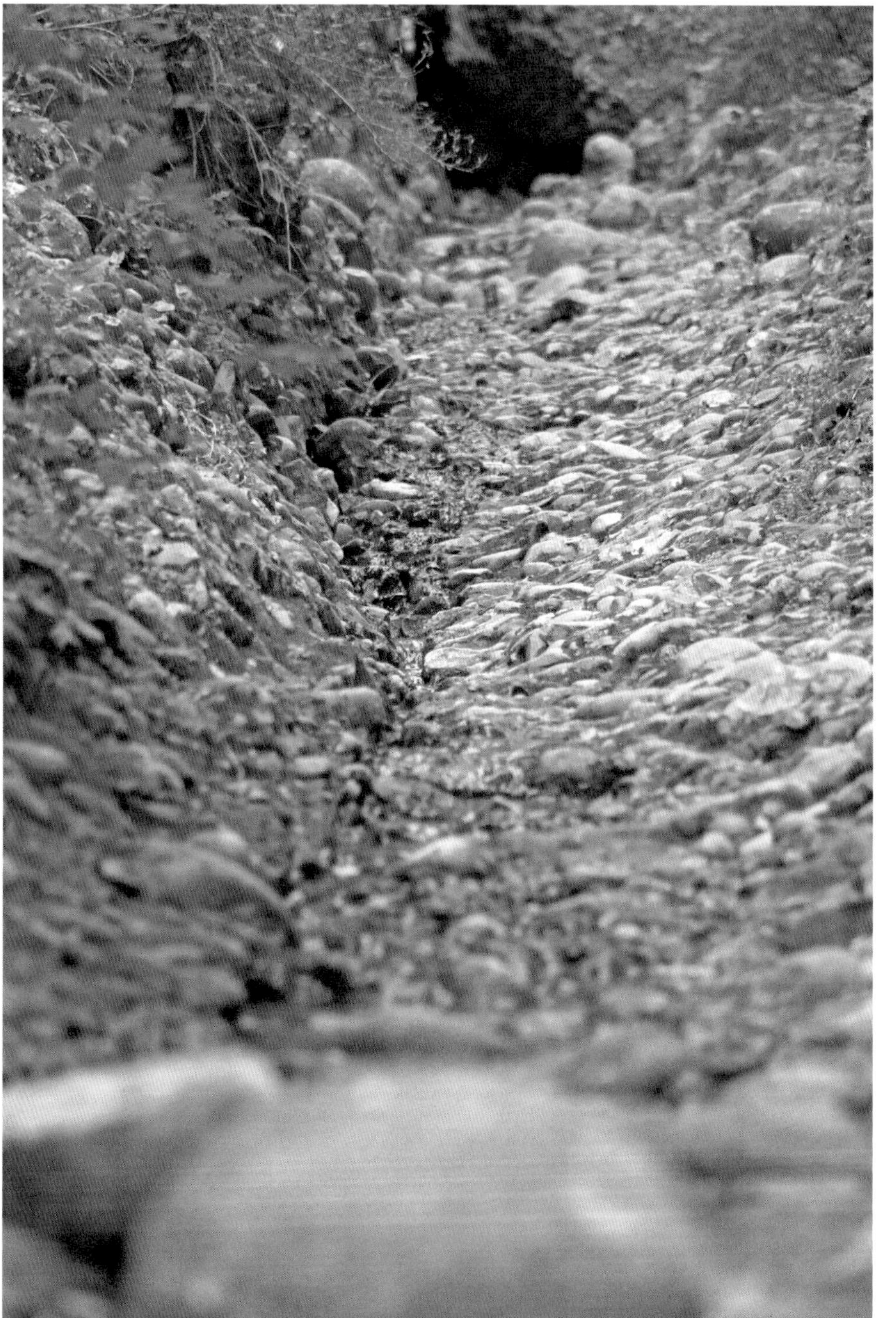

A stream runs down Box Canyon at Maple Canyon. *Author photo.*

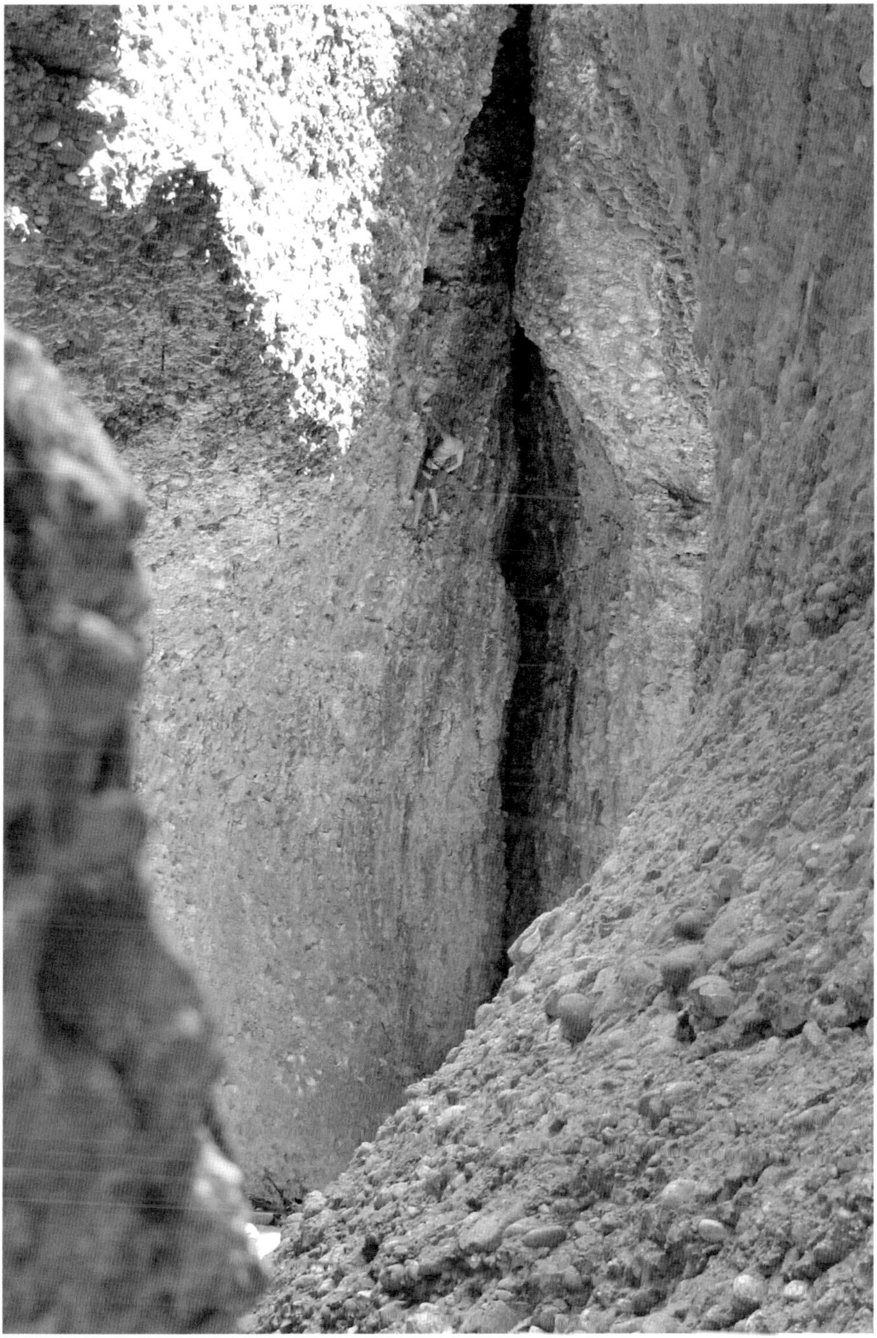

Megan Tierney climbs *Devil's Play Thing* in the Box Canyon at Maple Canyon. *Author photo.*

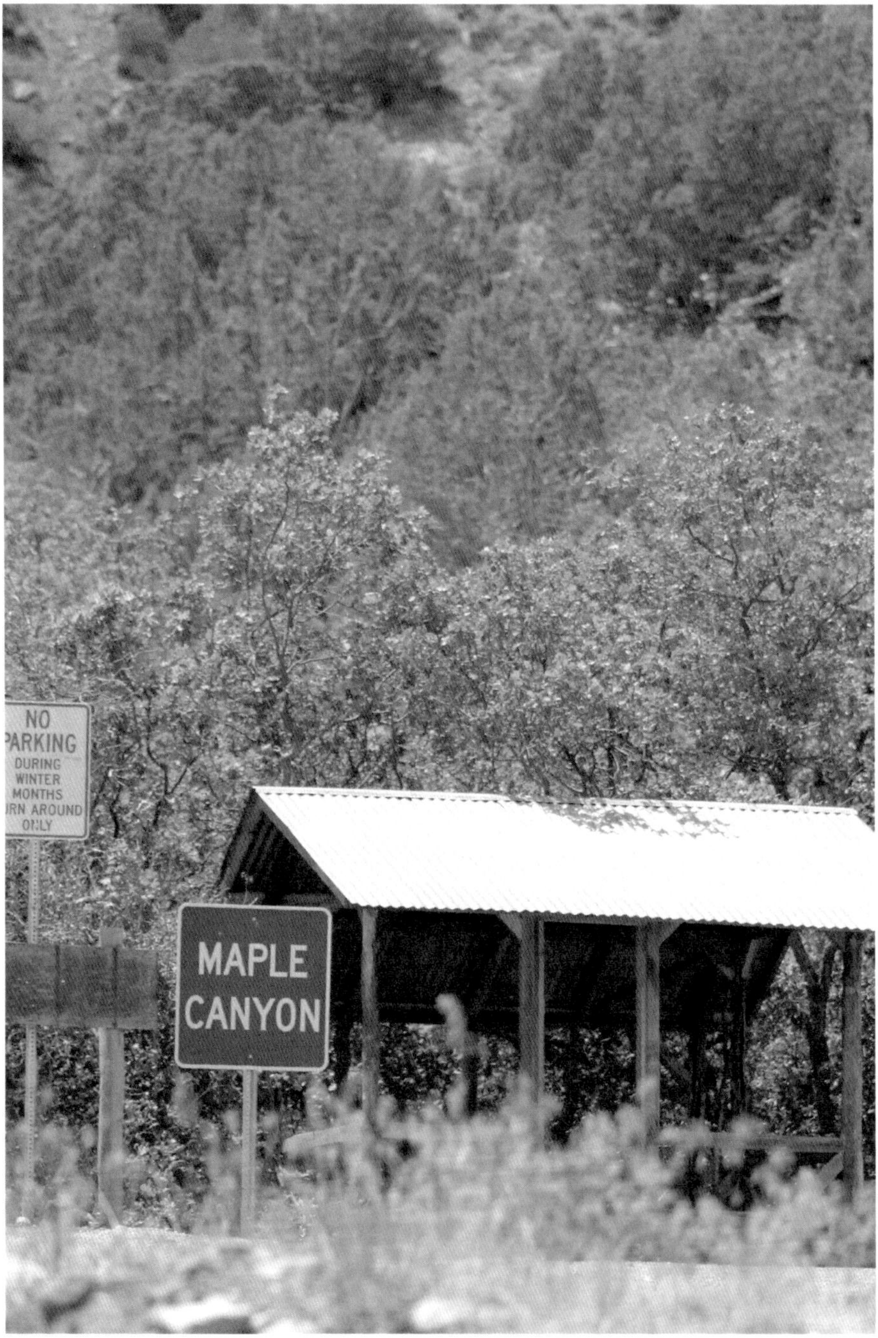

An entrance sign sits at the opening to Maple Canyon. *Author photo.*

In the summer of 1994, Pedersen, Boyle and their friend Knezek traveled south to visit a Mountainworks patron from Manti, Utah. That contact had been raving to them about a limestone canyon down in that area. So, the group finally consented and made the trip to Juab County. According to both Pedersen and Boyle, they immediately knew the canyon was no good. "It was all thirty to thirty-five feet, really just stuff to set up top ropes on," remembered Boyle. For part of the group that had just developed what was, at the time, the steepest, most difficult stuff in the country in American Fork Canyon, I imagine that type of development held no draw.

Seeming a little embarrassed, the patron added, almost as an afterthought, that there was this other little canyon that might be worth checking out. Pedersen, Boyle and Knezek decided it was worth the stop, so the group extended their afternoon and soon found themselves in Maple Canyon.

When Boyle first entered the canyon, his mind didn't go to climbing. "It was like you'd walked into another eon, another era. Like we were in some prehistoric place." And it does have that feeling. There is something in the way that the stone wraps around you, reaching over your head in gentle arcs that creates a completely immersive experience. I've been in canyons all through the state of Utah. I have my personal favorites, Logan Canyon and American Fork Canyon among them, but there is no canyon in this state or anywhere else I've been that so thoroughly removes you from our world. It is an entirely transporting experience. The air is comfortably chilled on a good day, and sounds, even small ones, carry a different weight as they bounce between the canyon's cobblestone walls. The stones, a mix of colors, from purple and blue to red, play off the green of the moss that grows everywhere. The light that makes it into the canyon seems to create a permanent magic hour—you know, that hour just before dawn or dusk when the lighting is perfect for photographers. I spent an entire day shooting in that canyon and didn't have one moment that was anything other than perfect lighting.

The sight of the cobblestone cliffs frightened the group of climbers at first. They were certain that they could pull one stone out and the whole mountain would come tumbling down around them. I'm certain they aren't the first or last people to feel this way. But as they tested the stone, they were shocked by how solid it was. These giant waves of stones were made for climbing.

The group would come back regularly over the next few months. Pedersen and Ohran took turns, one holding down the fort at Mountainworks, the other developing routes with the rest of the group in Maple.

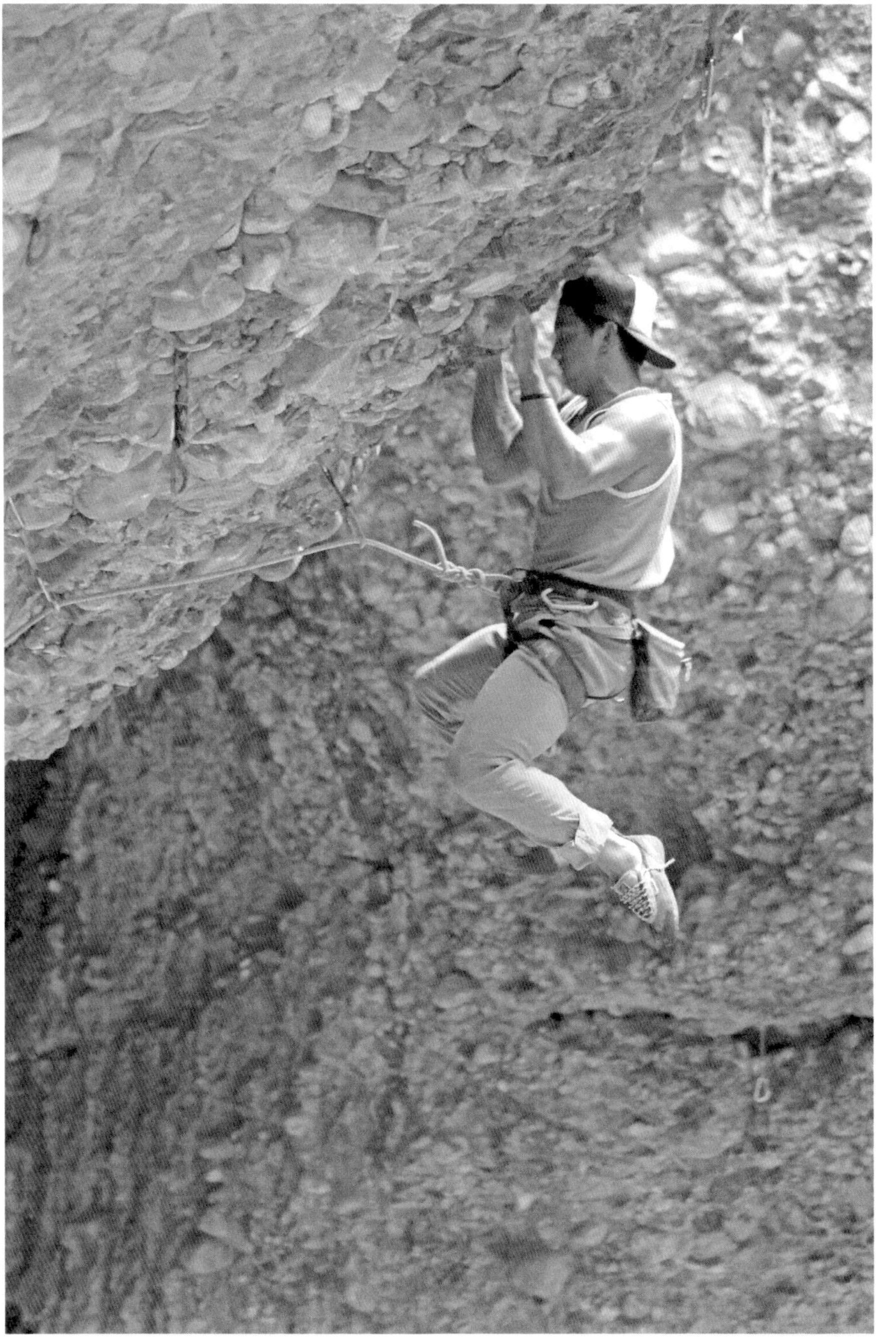

Metro Asunción at the crux of Ammo Dump in the Box Canyon at Maple Canyon. *Author photo.*

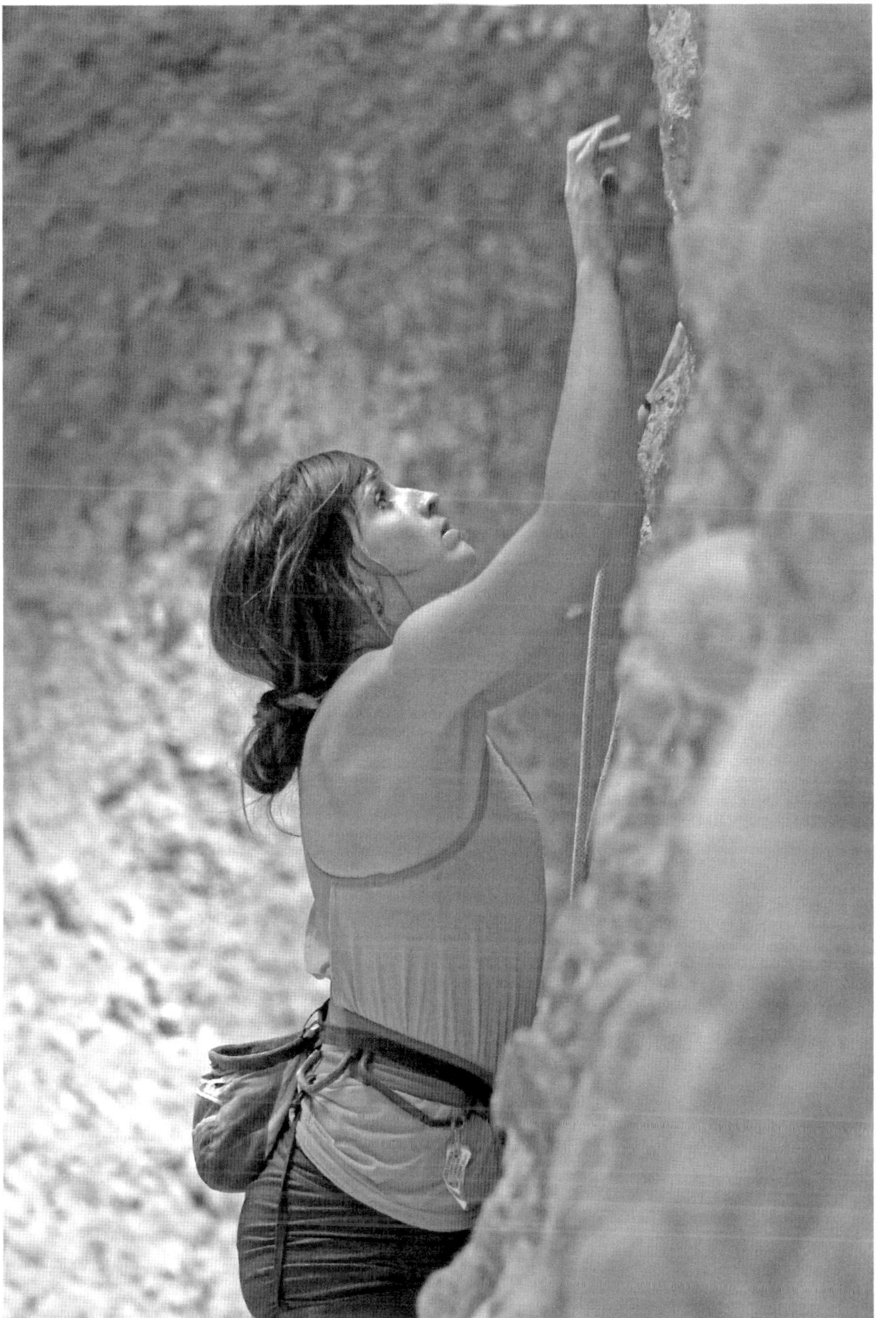

Jessica Powell climbs *Grip Tease* in the Box Canyon at Maple Canyon. *Author photo.*

Drilling bolts became its own problem. According to Boyle, some of the stones were so dense that you could barely get a drill to scratch them. There were also a lot of testing stones. While it wasn't often that one of the cobbles would pull loose, the threat posed by those few that would was severe enough for everyone working on the canyon to double check everything around the routes they were developing. The last thing any of them wanted was for a fellow climber to take a bad fall when a hold pulled off, and given the weight of most of the stones, it'd be even worse to imagine one of them striking a belayer or passing hiker.

Like I said at the beginning of this chapter, that's the story you'll get from the majority of the people you ask about the development of Maple Canyon. It is not, however, the whole story or even its beginning.

During my interview with Pedersen, he mentioned that he thought someone from nearby Snow College had taken students in there and done some climbing. Boyle confirmed this fact when he mentioned that as they explored the canyon, they did stumble on one or two existing routes.

Following up as best as I could, I decided to try to contact any sort of outdoor recreation department that Snow College might have. It had been decades since whoever put those routes in had done them, and I doubted that any one at Snow would remember them. But often this is how research goes. You jump from one long shot to another until you find a little hold that you can start to move from. After about a half hour of being bounced between departments (colleges and universities may not be the most well organized of institutions, but they are always more than happy to transfer you to a different department), I ended up speaking to the closest thing Snow has to an outdoor recreation department. A very friendly man named Roger told me that what I had heard was correct and that the person I wanted to talk to was Jason Stevens. According to Roger, Jason had done quite a bit of work climbing in Maple Canyon well before anyone else got in there.

It turns out he was right. Stevens actually started climbing when he was eight or nine years old. His father owned a painting business that had the contract for painting some of the Latter-day Saints temples. They would rig up ropes and harnesses and then work their way up and down the building. On weekends, Stevens and his father would take the gear and rappel off anything they could find, including the local water tank. Eventually, they started taking their rappelling gear camping, where they'd lower off cliffs. Before long, Stevens decided that going up might be more fun than going down, and he began his affair with rock climbing.

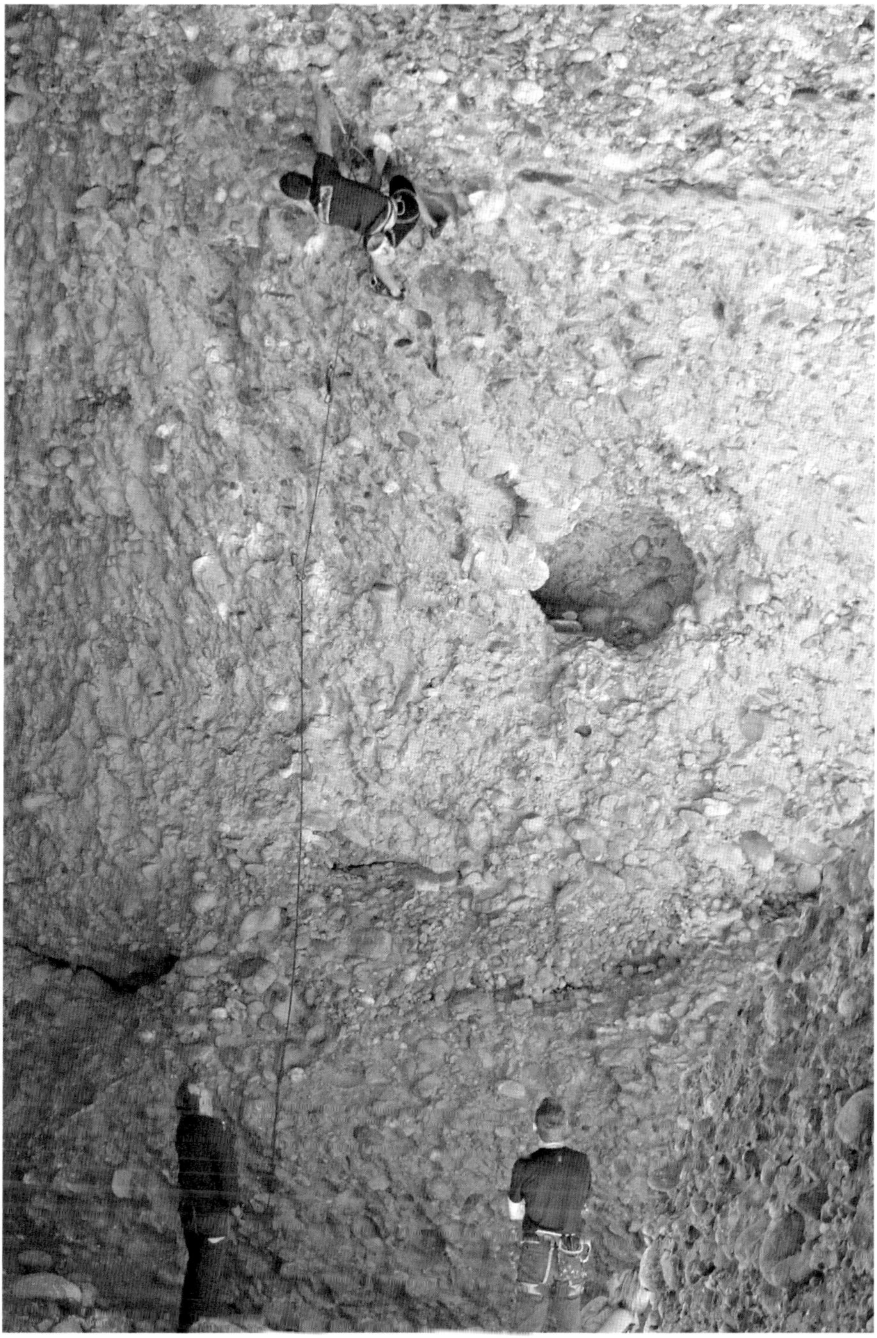

Heath Christensen climbs *In the Mean Time* in the Box Canyon at Maple Canyon. *Author photo.*

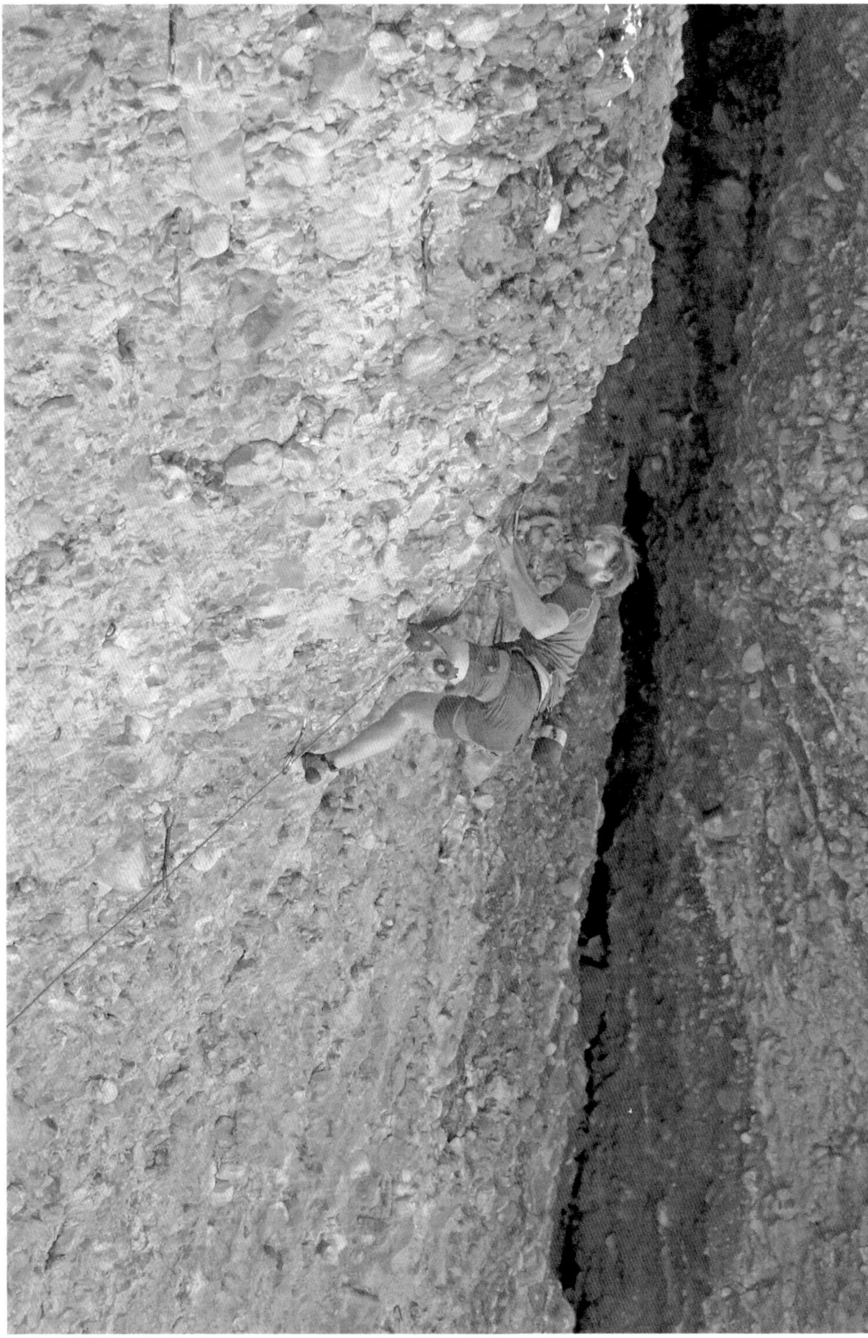

Derek Trepanier leads a climb in the Box Canyon at Maple Canyon. *Author photo.*

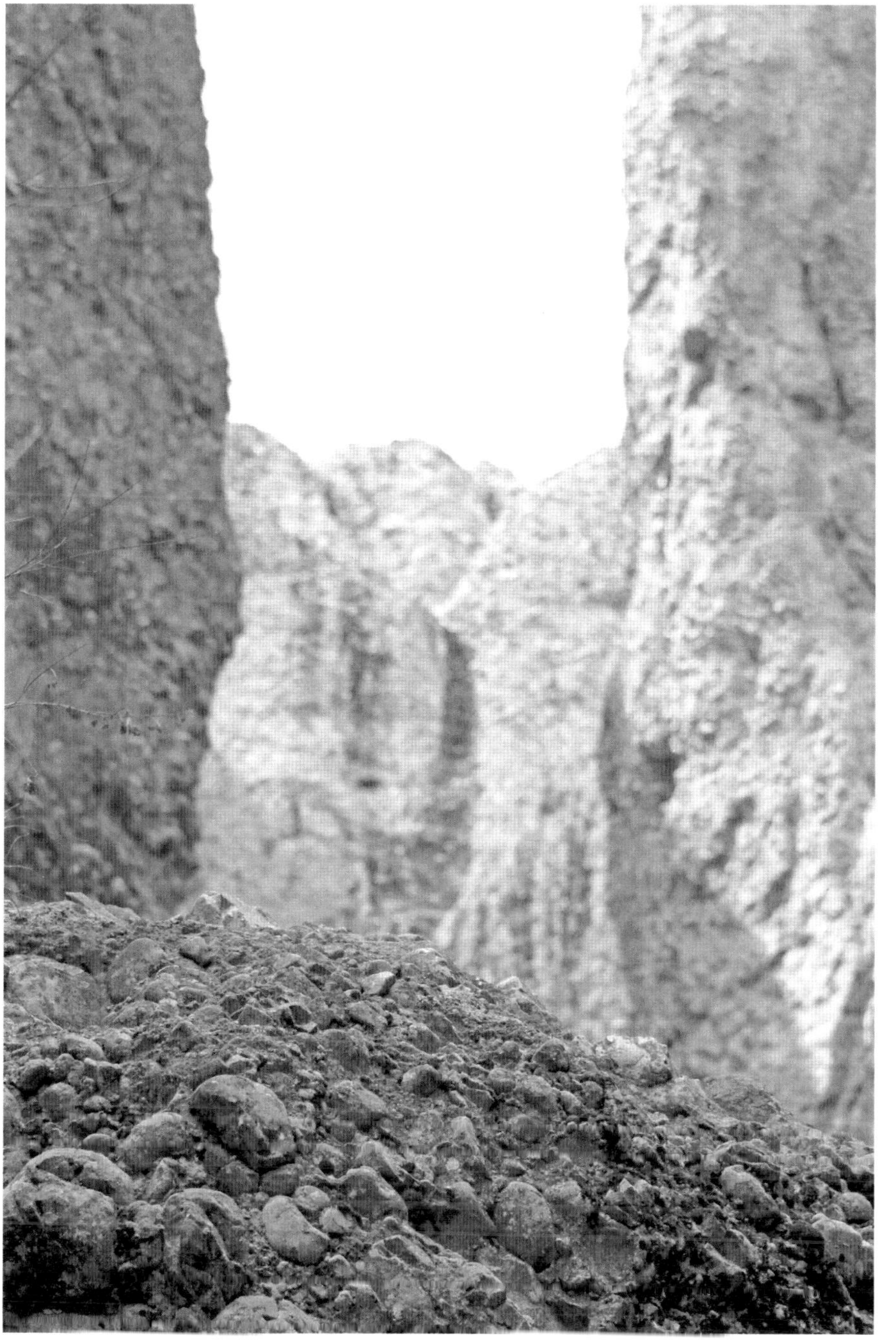

Picture of cobbles in the Box Canyon at Maple Canyon. *Author photo.*

Really, Stevens learned to climb in a bubble. Despite everything that was happening elsewhere in the state, he didn't meet another climber (or even know about the broader climbing community) until he'd been climbing for nearly a decade and had established several routes of his own. Without any knowledge of what the French and Italians were doing, without building on their example, Stevens took a diamond-shaped mason bit and chiseled the bolt holes for his first batch of routes.

That bubble started to pop in 1987–88, when a couple of Environmental Protection Agency employees from Colorado received an assignment in Sanpete County. Climbers, the two men asked around for information on any locals who could show them the area's crags. Eventually, they were directed to Stevens. To this point, Stevens hadn't done any climbing in Maple. Mostly, he'd developed in Axhandle Canyon and New Canyon (both in Sanpete County). At least in part, his hesitancy to climb in Maple seems to have stemmed from his earliest memories of the canyon.

During 1983–84, the area received record snowpack followed by an extra warm spring. This led to some of the worst flooding Sanpete County had seen. Maple Canyon took a direct hit. The road that had been built in the canyon was washed out from bottom to top. Mud had covered everything, and nature began to take back over. When Stevens made his first boyhood visit to the canyon, he saw it as "just a canyon with a wash in it." He remembers seeing Maple trees that had grown through the cracks in old picnic tables. It left the impression that Maple Canyon was an absolutely wild place.

Thinking that these "real" climbers from Colorado might be up to the challenge, he showed them the way to Maple Canyon. The two men had brought a hand drill with them, and for the first time, Stevens had an example of how bolting could be done. The trio put two bolts at the top of Antigravity Rock. They lowered from them and worked on the route that would become *Back to Zero* (5.11c, FA Jason Stevens).[15] Like most of Maple Canyon, Antigravity Rock is steep and overhung. As the group tried to make it up the route on top rope, which was beyond their abilities at the time, each fall sent them swinging out away from the rock face. Unable to swing back to the spot they'd fallen from, they'd have to lower to the ground and start from zero all over again.

Both as thanks and because they saw him as someone with potential, the two Colorado climbers left Stevens with an old pair of EB climbing shoes. They were the first pair he'd ever owned.

Getting his first glance outside the bubble he'd taught himself to climb in left Stevens with a renewed motivation and fire for climbing. He'd take his friends and ditch school to go climbing and route developing. As he put it, "You get that itch, and you just can't scratch it enough." This continued until Stevens left to serve on a two-year LDS mission.

When he returned, he picked up right where he left off. Years earlier, Stevens's father had traded the painting business for a general construction business that focused on steel buildings. Before long, Stevens had the ingenious idea of taking one of the company trucks with a big ol' arc welding generator, a corded drill, about six hundred feet of extension cords and a forty-foot extension ladder to one of Maple's roadside cliffs (the road having been rebuilt). "I had no idea what I was doing. Scared the crap out of me," Stevens confessed. Leaning the extension ladder against the cliff, he took the drill and began work on his first drilled sport route. At the time, Maple Canyon wasn't the popular place that it is now; in fact, it's quite possible he would have had the place all to himself—which was good since, as he put it, the generator "was ungodly loud." He named the route *Raindrops on Lichen* (5.9, FA Jason Stevens) and decided not to develop that way again. Instead, he hocked his snowboard at a local pawnshop and used the money to buy his first cordless drill, a Bosch Bulldog. With the Bulldog in tow, he would develop with even greater intensity. In total, Stevens had put in thirty to forty routes by the end of 1993.

In the spring of 1994, Stevens took a trip north to Provo, Utah, with some friends to go climbing in Rock Canyon. While they were in the area, they stopped by Mountainworks to purchase some gear. A couple months later, when Stevens returned to Maple Canyon, he was astonished to find what looked like forty routes in Box Canyon. The epic development done by the Utah County crew had made its way to Maple.

Inspiration to create doesn't require a community. Many artists have thrived on their own. As Stevens put it, he "did it largely alone and largely isolated from the rest of the world." Still, there is something about joining up with a community, collaborating and working with others, that breaths extra life into those creative fires. Sometimes, it takes the best of both scenarios to create something as astounding as the collection of climbs now featured in Maple Canyon.

GLOSSARY OF CLIMBING TERMS

A

aid climbing: A form of rock climbing where gear like pitons might be placed not only in the rock for protection but also as an aid in climbing the route.

approach: The path or trail that leads to a crag, wall or specific climb. It can be anywhere from a roadside approach that requires no walking to a lengthy and hazardous hike/scramble.

B

barn-door: To swing out from the wall attached by only two points of contact.

belay: To protect a climber by having the rope run through a climbing device, such as a Grigri, ATC or Figure 8, used to create friction and stop the climber's fall.

beta: Information on a climb, such as where difficult moves might be, how to work past certain sections or where to place gear.

bolt: A protection point that is meant to be permanent (though upkeep is required), created by drilling a hole into the rock and attaching any of several types of metal hanger or rings for climbers to clip their rope onto.

C

cam: A spring-loaded piece of rock-climbing protection where a number of cams are mounted on one or two axles so that force pulling on the protection causes the device to spread apart and jam in place.

carabiner: An oval metal ring used to connect objects by means of a spring-loaded gate.

chopping bolts: The intentional act of removing a climber's bolt/s from a wall.

choss: Loose rock of a poor quality.

circuit: A short series of climbing moves, usually done on a loop for training purposes.

clean climb: A climb that can be completed without the aid of equipment, like a piton, for anything other than protection.

crag: One small, contained area of rock climbing. A canyon will contain many crags.

crimp: (verb) to maximize the force that can be placed on the tips of the fingers by positioning the fingers in a particular technique; (noun) a very small rock feature, usually only large enough to fit the tips of a climber's fingers.

crux: The most challenging portion of a climb.

D

decking: Falling from a climb and hitting the ground.

dynamic rope: A rope with a bit of elasticity to it, which absorbs some of the force of a climber's fall.

E

Elvis legs: The condition when a climber's leg/s begin to shake uncontrollably due to tiredness or nerves.

exposure: The empty space around a climber.

F

face climbing: Rock climbing done on a section of rock containing no cracks or features large enough in which to place traditional protection.

figure-eight knot: A commonly used knot that attaches a rope to a climber's harness.

first ascent: Credit given to the first climber (usually but not always the route developer) to red-point the climb.

free soloing: A form of climbing where the climber uses no rope or protection. As opposed to bouldering, free-soloing routes are similar in length to sport or trad routes.

friction (also known as smearing): A climbing move that relies on the friction between the sole of the climber's shoe/s and the rock as opposed to placing a toe or portion of the foot on a feature of the rock.

G

gaston: A climbing technique where the climber uses one or two hands to pull on a vertical feature/s outward from his or her body. Picture trying to pry an elevator door open.

ground fall: A fall, or the threat of a fall, where the protection is placed in such a way that hitting the ground, or decking, becomes a possibility even with appropriate belaying.

ground up: Bolting a climbing route on lead, placing protection and bolts on the way up.

H

harness: A piece of climbing equipment worn around the waist and thighs that connects to a rope and allows the climber to hang (or catch a fall) on the rope.

high step: A climbing technique where climbers place their foot on a feature at or near their waist.

I

ice climbing: The process of climbing up a section of ice using tools designed for the activity.

J

jug: A large hand hold that is easily grasped.

L

lead climbing: A form of climbing (trad or sport) where climbers pull the rope up with them (attached to their harness) and either place protection they then clip into or clip the rope into an existing bolt using a quickdraw.

locking carabiner: A carabiner with a gate that can be locked closed.

M

micro wires: A very small—usually smaller than a quarter—form of trad climbing gear placed into a rock feature for protection.

mixed-gear route (mixed-aid route): A route that requires both trad gear (like nuts or cams) and sport gear (like quickdraws) in order to complete the climb. These routes are usually found when a blank section of stone either blocks the start of the route or appears between two sections of the route.

multi-pitch: A climbing route that is too long for a single rope.

N

no-hand rest: A position that allows climbers to have both arms off the wall while resting (usually where all the climbers' weight is on their legs).

nut: A medium to large metallic rectangle threaded on a wire that is wedged in a rock feature in trad climbing to halt climbers' falls.

O

onsite: To free climb a route on one's first attempt, having no prior knowledge or information about the route and not having seen anyone else attempt it.

P

pitch: One section of a rock-climbing route (trad or sport). Often marked by a set of chains where belayer and climber can trade duties to move up a longer route.

piton: A metal spike hammered into a rock as a point of protection should the climber fall.

project: A route that has not yet had its first ascent.

pump(ed): The condition when a climbers' forearms are so tired that gripping even simple holds becomes extremely difficult or impossible.

Q

quickdraw: Two carbiners connected by a small stretch of webbing. They are used in sport climbing to connect the rope to a bolt.

R

rap bolting: Bolting a climbing route while secured on rappel, as opposed to bolting from the ground up on lead.

rappel: To descend on a fixed rope using any number of friction devices.

rebolting: The process of replacing old, worn-out bolts on an existing climb. Also, the process of replacing bolts after they have been chopped.

red-point: To free climb a route that one has attempted at least one time previously.

retro bolting: Adding bolts to a previously established trad climb.

roof: A section of rock that reaches or nearly reaches horizontal.

route: The path up a section of rock.

runout: A route or section of a route (trad or sport) where the space between protection points is great enough as to make the climb dangerous, often, though not always, with the possibility of a ground fall (or decking)

S

sandbag: A climb that is rated easier than it actually is.

side pulling: Gripping a hold sideways and pulling toward the body.

sloper: A hold that requires climbers to use an open hand, like palming a basketball.

smearing: *See* friction

T

top-rope: To climb a route on belay from a rope that has previously been secured at the top of the climb. Thus, the climber is protected from falling at any moment during the climb.

traditional (or trad) climbing: A form of climbing where the route contains no pre-established protection, such as bolts. All protection must be placed in natural rock features by climbers as they move up the route.

traverse: To climb in a horizontal direction.

U

undercling: (verb) to grab a hold with an upward-facing palm; (noun) a hold that must be grabbed with an upward-facing palm.

W

webbing: A flat strip of nylon cord.

whipper: A sizable fall while lead climbing (trad or sport), often from above and to the side of the last protection point, causing climbers to whip sideways as they fall.

X

X-rated: A climb that has so little protection or where the protection is so far apart (runout) that a fall could result in serious injury or death.

Y

Yosemite decimal system: A U.S.-based numerical rating system for the difficulty of hikes and climbs. The easiest starts at 5.0. After 5.10, ratings are further divided by letter (so, a 5.10c is one grade more difficult than a 5.10b). It is the most common rating system used in the States.

Z

Z-clip: To clip into a bolt or piece of trad gear using a segment of rope from below the previous bolt or piece of gear. This creates a tangle that is both dangerous and makes movement up the route impossible.

NOTES

1. Raleigh, "John Bachar's Last Interview."
2. Garrett, *Utah's West Desert*, 68.
3. Ruckman and Ruckman, *Rock Climbing the Wasatch Range*, 199, 216.
4. Garrett, *Utah's West Desert*, 3.
5. Raleigh, "Ron Olevsky Files," 39.
6. Ibid., 38.
7. Shelley, *Early History of American Fork.*
8. Ruckman and Ruckman, *Climber's Guide*, 86.
9. Ibid., 85.
10. Bushman, interview, 19–22.
11. Hyer, *Northern Utah Limestone Climbing*, 57.
12. Hecht, *Doubt*, xvii.
13. Ruckman and Ruckman, *Rock Climbing the Wasatch Range*, 199.
14. Ibid., 209.
15. Pegg, Hechtel and Holmes, *Maple Canyon Rock Climbs*, 17.

BIBLIOGRAPHY

Adams, Vince. Interview by Darren M. Edwards, 2007.

Andersen, Michael. Interview by Darren M. Edwards, 2016.

Atwell, Susan Bosse. Interview by Darren M. Edwards, 2015.

Bigwood, Noah. Interview by Darren M. Edwards, 2016.

Boyle, Bill. Interview by Darren M. Edwards, 2015.

Bushman, Scott. Interview by Brad Cole and Darren M. Edwards. In *Land Use Management Oral History Project*. Edited by Brad Cole and Darren M. Edwards, 19–22. Logan, UT: Mountain West Center for Regional Studies, 2008.

Cupal, Matt. Interview by Darren M. Edwards, 2016.

Datwyler, Scott. Interview by Darren M. Edwards, 2016.

Driscoll, Matt. *Outdoor Recreation History*. Salt Lake City: University of Utah, 2010.

Garrett, James. Interview by Darren M. Edwards, 2015.

———. *Utah's West Desert*. N.p.: James Garrett, 2011.

Goss, Todd. Interview by Darren M. Edwards, 2016.

———. *Rock Climbs of Southwest Utah and the Arizona Strip*. Boulder, CO: Sharp End Publishing, 2006.

Hathaway, Lisa. Interview by Darren M. Edwards 2016.

Hecht, Jennifer Michael. *Doubt: A History*. New York: HarperCollins, 2003.

Hyer, Casey. *Northern Utah Limestone Climbing*. Boulder, CO: Sharp End Publishing, 2004.

Ibach, John. Interview by Darren M. Edwards, 2015.

Kelley, Casey. *High on Moab*. Boulder, CO: Sharp End Publishing, 2014.

Ohran, Bill. Interview by Darren M. Edwards, 2015.

Pedersen, Jeff. Interview by Darren M. Edwards, 2015.

Pegg, Dave, Sibylle Hechtel and Josh Holmes. *Maple Canyon Rock Climbs*. New Castle, CO: Wolverine Publishing, 2012.

Pleinis, Mike. Interview by Darren M. Edwards, 2015.

Raleigh, Duane. "John Bachar's Last Interview." *Rock and Ice* (online version). http://www.rockandice.com/lates-news/john-bachar-rock-climbing-purist?page=1.

———. "The Ron Olevsky Files." *Rock and Ice* 132 (April 2004): 36–41.

Robb, David. Interview by Darren M. Edwards, 2015.

———. *Ogden Area Climbing Guide*. Boulder, CO: Sharp End Publising, 2005.

Ruckman, Brett, and Stuart Ruckman. *Climber's Guide to American Fork Canyon and Rock Canyon*. Guilford, CT: Globe Pequot Press, 1995.

———. *Rock Climbing the Wasatch Range*. Guilford, CT: Falcon, 1998.

Shelley, George F. *An Early History of American Fork with Some History of a Later Day*. American Fork City, CO: American Fork City, 1993.

Speed, Boone. Interview by Darren M. Edwards, 2015.

Stevens, Jason. Interview by Darren M. Edwards, 2016.

ABOUT THE AUTHOR

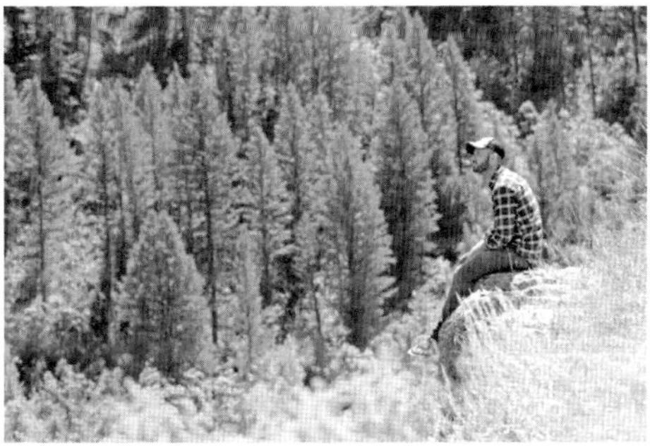

Darren M. Edwards is a writer. Sometimes he writes poems. Sometimes he writes prose. Sometimes he just writes strings of obscenities. He started sport climbing in American Fork Canyon during high school. Later, while attending Utah State University in Logan, Utah, where he earned both a bachelor's degree in English and a master's degree in literature and writing, he spent nearly a decade sport climbing up Logan Canyon. After moving to southern Utah to teach courses at Dixie State University, Darren spent two years serving as the slam master for southern Utah's slam poetry community, during which time he was also a member of two national poetry slam teams. He has a wife, a dog and a little squishy person they're calling a son. In the real world of bills and money, Darren currently works as the managing editor for the *Southern Utah Independent*, where he also writes a biweekly opinion column. Outside of that, his work has been published in places like *Urban Climber*, *Dialogue*, *Camas* and *Stone Voices*, among others.